FEDERAL ESTATE AND GIFT TAXATION

Eighth Edition

REVISED STUDY PROBLEMS
Second Revision

RICHARD B. STEPHENS
Late Professor Emeritus
University of Florida

STEPHEN A. LIND
Albert R. Abramson Distinguished Professor of Law
Hastings College of Law

DENNIS A. CALFEE
Professor of Law
University of Florida

WG&L

THOMSON REUTERS
117 East Stevens Avenue
Valhalla, NY 10595

ISBN: 978-0-7913-7256-2

PRINTED IN THE UNITED STATES OF AMERICA

INTRODUCTION

If as a student you are getting into these sets of problems, it is most likely because an instructor has directed you to work them, and that instructor's direction was accompanied by further instruction regarding objectives and procedures. Should you perchance be using these study problems on your own, you may find the following brief remarks of some interest.

It is nearly impossible to learn a statutory area of the law merely by reading, even by carefully studying the statute. Such reading and study are essential, but not enough. Examining what others say about the statute, whether the others be the government, through their regulations and rulings, or the authors of this treatise, is still not enough. Studying what the courts have said about the statute in a great variety of concrete settings may bring us closer to some comprehension. Sound research requires this approach to specific problems in practice, and, if it did not involve such an extravagant use of time, this Langdelian case method might still result in good education.

The problems presented here are a kind of substitute for the examination and analysis of large numbers of cases. They ask you to look at the various statutory provisions in context and to consider relationships of various concepts. An instructor's guidance or questioning is very helpful in this activity, but much can be accomplished without it, perhaps with some assistance from the treatise.

Regarding some of the problems, you will not "know you know" the answers. Welcome to the club; there are areas of uncertainty. You should, however, be able to grasp the basic concepts sufficiently so that the federal transfer taxes are not strangers to you—so that you can think about them in complete sentences or paragraphs, so to speak, and not just in terms of isolated words or phrases. This is what basic tax study is all about. It is a beginning, a necessary first hurdle, upon which, with "practice" (and apt word for us professionals), knowledge and perception can expand.

TABLE OF CONTENTS

PROBLEM 1

[SMLC&S refers to the abridged edition of Federal Estate and Gift Taxation (8th ed.). Appendix begins on page 103 of the Study Problems.]

Assignment

Code: In the final analysis, estate planning must include a consideration of all taxes, state and federal, since the surprise exaction of a tax may upset expectations that are otherwise reasonable. Here, however, consideration is limited to the federal transfer taxes, the estate tax, the gift tax, and the generation-skipping transfer tax. This assignment explores the basic computational relationship of those three taxes. The Code sections principally to be examined are:

§§ 2001(a)–2001(c); 2010(a), 2010(c); 2501(a)(1); 2502(a); 2505(a); 2601; 2602; 2611(a); 2622; 2641.

SMLC&S: Preface; ¶¶ 2.01[2]–2.01[3]. Skim ¶¶ 1.01–1.06.

Appendix: Applicable Credit Amount Table

Questions

(1) *T*, never having made any prior inter vivos gifts, made *taxable gifts* of $2 million in 2005. *T* dies in the current year, leaving a *taxable estate* of $3 million.

In 1992, *G* created a trust, the income to be paid to *G*'s child *T* (our same good old *T*) for life, remainder to *T*'s child *R*. (Don't worry about *G* who is not a part of the problem.) At *T*'s death in the current year, the remainder interest of the trust corpus, valued at $4 million, was paid over to *R*.

(a) Using the proper rate computation provided by Section 2502 and considering the Section 2505 applicable credit amount (see the Applicable Credit Amount Table in the Appendix), what is *T*'s gift tax liability for 2005?

(b) Determine the estate tax payable on *T*'s death in the current year, using the Section 2001 computation and the Section 2010 applicable credit amount. See the Applicable Credit Amount Table in the Appendix.

(c) Consider the Section 2001(b) statutory method for computation of estate tax liability: Are the "taxable gifts" being taxed twice? What is being taxed? How?

(d) Proper computations in both questions **(1)(a)** and **(1)(b)**, above, make use of the applicable credit amount. Is the credit allowed twice?

(e) Using an inclusion ratio equal to one and a taxable amount equal to the value of the remainder interest, what is the amount of tax imposed on the taxable termination generation-skipping transfer that occurs upon *T*'s death?

PROBLEM 2

[SMLC&S refers to the abridged edition of Federal Estate and Gift Taxation (8th ed.). Appendix begins on page 103 of the Study Problems.]

Assignment

Code:	§§ 2031(a); 2033; 2034. Skim §§ 691(a); 1014(a), 1014(c); 7520.
Regulations:	§§ 20.2031-1(a), 20.2031-1(b); 20.2033-1; 20.2034-1. Skim § 20.2031-6.
SMLC&S:	¶¶ 4.01; 4.02[1]–4.02[2][a]; 4.05 (omit ¶ 4.05[8]); 4.06.
Appendix:	Table S.
Suggested references:	Goodman v. Granger, 243 F2d 264 (3d Cir. 1957), 57-1 USTC ¶ 11,687, 51 AFTR 67, cert. denied, 355 US 835 (1957).
	Rev. Rul. 75-127, 1975-1 CB 297.
	Smith v. Shaughnessy, 318 US 176 (1943), 43-1 USTC ¶ 10,013, 30 AFTR 388.

Questions

(1) *D* transferred property to *T*, as trustee, in trust, the income to be paid to *X* for *X*'s life, remainder to *Y* if living at *X*'s death or, if not, remainder to *Z* or *Z*'s estate.

(a) If *T* died, survived by *X*, would the value of the property be included in *T*'s gross estate?

(b) Will the value of the property be included in *X*'s gross estate upon *X*'s death? Is any wealth transfer tax possibly applicable upon *X*'s death?

(c) Will a part of the value of the property be included in *Y*'s gross estate if *Y* dies survived by *X*?

(d) Will a part of the value of the property be included in *Z*'s gross estate if *Z* dies survived by *X* but not by *Y*? In the current year, what amount, if any, would be included in *Z*'s gross estate if the trust corpus is worth $100,000, *X* is 60 years old, the Section 7520(a)(2) interest rate is 4 percent, and *Z*'s estate uses a date-of-death valuation? See Table S in the Appendix to the Study Problems.

(e) Will a part of the value of the property be included in *Z*'s gross estate if *Z* dies survived by *X* and *Y*?

(f) Will a part of the value of the property be included in Z's gross estate under the circumstances of question **(1)(d)**, above, if the trust was an inter vivos trust created by *D*, subject to *D*'s power of revocation, and *Z* was also survived by *D*?

(g) If *D* had made the transfer in question **(1)(a)**, above, but had provided for a reversion to *D* or *D*'s estate (rather than a remainder to *Z* or *Z*'s estate) if *Y* was not living at *X*'s death, will anything be included in *D*'s estate if *D* predeceases *X* and *Y*?

(2) Consider the extent to which state law may affect federal tax liability.

(a) *D* died owning a residence that is protected from the claims of creditors by the state's homestead law. Is the residence includable under Section 2033?

(b) Under state community property law, *D*'s spouse is the owner of one half of their community property during their lives and at the death of *D*. Is spouse's interest in such property a part of *D*'s gross estate? Note, however, IRC § 1014(b)(6).

(c) Under the law of a state that uses common law property concepts, *D*'s spouse became entitled at *D*'s death to one third of *D*'s realty and one third of *D*'s personalty outright. Are these interests a part of *D*'s gross estate?

(d) *D* and *D*'s spouse own property as equal tenants in common, which, under state law, involves no right of survivorship. Is any part of *D*'s interest included in *D*'s gross estate under Section 2033 if *D* dies survived by *D*'s spouse?

(e) What is the result in question **(2)(d)**, above, under Section 2033, if *D* and *D*'s spouse own the property as joint tenants or as tenants by the entirety and, under a decision by the state supreme court, the tenants enjoy rights of survivorship? What is the result if state courts disagree as to whether there is a right of survivorship and the state supreme court has not yet resolved the issue?

(3) *D*'s employer owed *D* $1,500 in salary that had not been paid at time of death.

- **(a)** Is *D*'s right to that amount includable in *D*'s gross estate?
- **(b)** For the estate's or beneficiary's income tax purposes, what difference may it make whether *D* was an accrual or a cash-method taxpayer? See IRC § 691, especially IRC § 691(c).
- **(c)** What if the $1,500 is a benefit that *D*'s employer agreed to pay to *D* or *D*'s estate only if *D* continued to work for the employer until *D*'s retirement or death, and *D* works until the day *D* dies?
- **(d)** If the $1,500 is a benefit that *D*'s employer is not required by contract to pay, but that the employer decides to pay all employees at the end of the year, and if *D* dies during the year and the amount is paid to *D*'s estate, is the benefit included in *D*'s gross estate under Section 2033?
- **(e)** Are Social Security benefits paid to *D*'s family at *D*'s death includable in *D*'s gross estate under Section 2033?

(4) *D* dies owning a real estate business.

- **(a)** What is included in *D*'s gross estate under Section 2033 if the business is unincorporated?
- **(b)** What is included if the business is incorporated?
- **(c)** What if *D* owns a one-fourth interest in the business, which is a partnership in which the other three-fourths interest is owned by unrelated persons?

(5) At *D*'s death, which of the following are included in *D*'s gross estate under Section 2033?

- **(a)** A life insurance policy owned by *D* on *B*'s life. *B* survives *D*.
- **(b)** *B*'s survivorship rights in a joint and survivorship annuity policy for *D* and *B*'s lives purchased by *D*.
- **(c)** An installment sales obligation from the sale of property that *D* sold a few years ago.

PROBLEM 3

[SMLC&S refers to the abridged edition of Federal Estate and Gift Taxation (8th ed.).]

Assignment

Code:	§§ 2035; 2043(a). Skim § 2042.
Regulations:	§ 20.2043-1(a).
SMLC&S:	¶¶ 4.07 (omit ¶¶ 4.07[2][b][ii], 4.07[2][d], 4.07[4]); 4.15[2].
Suggested reference:	Rev. Rul. 72-282, 1972-1 CB 306.

Questions

(1) Two years ago, Decedent gave Child $75,000 in cash. Decedent dies in the current year.

(a) What is included in Decedent's gross estate?

(b) What is the result in question **(1)(a)**, above, if Decedent gave Child a life insurance policy on Decedent's life worth $10,000, with a face value of $75,000, instead of cash?

(c) What is the result in question **(1)(b)**, above, if, after the gift, Child made annual premium payments totaling $3,000? Assume that Decedent's total pre-gift premium payments were $12,000.

(d) What is the result in question **(1)(b)**, above, if, during the time between the gift and Decedent's death, the insurance policy paid dividends to Child totaling $1,000?

(e) What amount is included in Decedent's gross estate if, between the gift and Decedent's death, Child cashes in the policy and receives $12,000?

(f) What amount is included in Decedent's gross estate if Child paid Decedent $10,000 for the policy when the policy was worth $10,000?

(g) What amount is included in Decedent's gross estate if Child paid Decedent $5,000 for the policy when the policy was worth $10,000?

(2) In year one, Deathly Ill made a $300,000 gift of cash to Child, and, in year two, Deathly paid a $125,000 gift tax on the transfer.

- **(a)** Upon Deathly's death later in year two, what is included in Deathly's gross estate under Section 2035?
- **(b)** If Deathly had held on and lived for four years after the gift, what would be included in Deathly's gross estate under Section 2035?
- **(c)** If Deathly had not made the gift (and, consequently, had not paid the $125,000 gift tax), what would be included in Deathly's gross estate?

(3) Question **(2)**, above, demonstrates one tax reason for making inter vivos gifts.

- **(a)** What additional tax reasons are there for making inter vivos gifts?
- **(b)** Assuming that the property to be gifted has appreciated in value since its acquisition, is there any income tax disadvantage to making an inter vivos gift of the property? What factors should one consider with respect to this disadvantage in determining whether to make an inter vivos gift of the property?
- **(c)** Assuming that the property to be gifted has depreciated in value since its acquisition, is there any income tax advantage to making an inter vivos gift of the property?

PROBLEM 4

[SMLC&S refers to the abridged edition of Federal Estate and Gift Taxation (8th ed.).]

Assignment

Code:	§§ 2035(a); 2036; 2043(a).
Regulations:	§ 20.2036-1.
Proposed Regulations:	§§ 20.2036-2(a), 20.2036-2(c), 20.2036-2(d)(1), 20.2036-2(e)(2).
SMLC&S:	¶ 4.08 (omit ¶¶ 4.08[6], 4.08[7][c], 4.08[9]).
Suggested references:	Estate of Alexander v. Comm'r, 81 TC 757 (1983), aff'd in an unpublished opinion (4th Cir. 1985).
	Estate of D'Ambrosio v. Comm'r, 101 F3d 309 (3d Cir. 1996), 96-2 USTC ¶ 60,252, 78 AFTR2d 7347.
	Estate of Maxwell v. Comm'r, 3 F3d 591 (2d Cir. 1993), 93-2 USTC ¶ 60,145, 72 AFTR2d 6733.
	Rev. Rul. 95-58, 1995-2 CB 191.
	United States v. Allen, 293 F2d 916 (10th Cir. 1961), 61-2 USTC ¶ 12,032, 8 AFTR2d 6055, cert. denied, 368 US 944 (1962).
	United States v. Grace, 395 US 316 (1969), 69-1 USTC ¶ 12,609, 23 AFTR2d 1954.
	United States v. O'Malley, 383 US 627 (1966), 66-1 USTC ¶ 12,388, 17 AFTR2d 1393.

Questions

(1) *D* transfers securities to a trust, retaining some right to the trust income for some period described in the subparts of this question. What does Section 2036 require to be included in *D*'s gross estate in the following alternative circumstances?

- **(a)** One half of the income is to be paid to *D* for *D*'s life, remainder to Child *C* or *C*'s estate.
- **(b)** All the income is to be paid to *D* annually, generally for *D*'s life, but *D* is entitled to no trust income earned in the three-month period preceding *D*'s death. The remainder and undistributed income is to be paid to Child *C* or *C*'s estate at *D*'s death.
- **(c)** All the income is to be paid to *D* for ten years, when the trust is to terminate and the corpus is to be distributed to Child *C* or *C*'s estate. *D* dies after nine years have elapsed.

(2) Several years ago, *D* created a trust under which the income was to be paid to *D*'s sibling, *S*, for *S*'s life, then to *D* for *D*'s life. Upon the death of the survivor of *D* and *S*, the corpus was to be distributed to *R* or *R*'s estate. At *D*'s death more than three years later, *D* was survived by *S* and *R*. The corpus of the trust was then worth $300,000, with *S* and *R*'s interests worth $100,000 and $200,000, respectively. What amount should be included in *D*'s gross estate?

(3) Grantor created a trust naming a bank as trustee. The trust income was to be expended equally for Grantor's two children toward their support during their minority, which under state law was age 21. As each child came of age, that child became entitled to receive the child's share of the trust income directly. Upon the death of each child, that child's share of the trust corpus was to be distributed equally among the child's children. The trust instrument contained suitable provisions for distribution of income and corpus in the case of premature death of a child or the child's death without children. Grantor died when one of the children was age 15 and the other 22. To what extent, if any, does Section 2036 apply to the transfer?

(4) Consider the Section 2036 consequences to Homeowner, *H*, who, in the alternative, does the following:

- **(a)** *H* transfers *H*'s residence to Child *C* for no consideration, and *H* continues to live in the residence until *H*'s death.
- **(b)** *H* transfers the residence to *C* for no consideration, and *H* leases the property from *C* at its fair market value.
- **(c)** *H* sells the residence to *C* for cash in an amount equal to its fair market value, and *H* continues to live in the residence until *H*'s death.
- **(d)** *H* sells the residence to *C* for an interest-only note with a face value

equal to the fair market value of the residence. Shortly after the sale, *H* executes a will that provides for forgiveness of the entire mortgage debt upon *H*'s death. *H* also forgives $13,000 of the principal obligation on an annual basis. *H* continues to live in the residence until *H*'s death pursuant to a lease entered into with *C* that provides for the rental of the residence at its fair rental value. At the time of the transfer the fair rental value and the interest obligation on the debt are close in amount.

(e) Same as question **(4)(d)**, above, except that the note provides for payments that are part interest and part principal.

(5) Grantor transfers $1 million to a trust that provides income to Grantor for life, with a remainder to Grantor's Child. On creation of the trust, the remainder interest is worth $400,000. Child transfers $400,000 of Child's own funds to Grantor to purchase the remainder. At Grantor's death, the corpus is worth $2 million. What amount is included in Grantor's gross estate?

(6) Grantor creates a trust with income to *X* or *X*'s estate *for Grantor's life*, and a remainder to *Y* or *Y*'s estate. Grantor predeceases *X* and *Y* (and *Z*, where *Z* appears in the subparts below). How, if at all, does Section 2036 apply in the following situations?

(a) Grantor, as trustee, retains a power to invade corpus for *Z*.

(b) Grantor, as trustee, retains a power to accumulate income and add it to corpus.

(c) Grantor, as trustee, retains a power to invade the corpus of the trust for *X*.

(d) Grantor names unrelated friend *E* trustee, and *E* holds a power to give income to *Z*.

(e) The facts are the same as in question **(6)(d)**, above, but Grantor also retains a power to remove *E* as trustee at any time and name Grantor trustee, holding all powers that *E* held.

(f) The facts are the same as in question **(6)(d)**, above, but Grantor names a corporate trustee and retains the right to remove the trustee without cause and to appoint another corporate trustee.

(g) Grantor names Grantor trustee and provides that the trustee is required to give *Z* as much income as is needed each year for *Z*'s support and maintenance, with any excess income to go to *X*.

(h) Grantor names unrelated friend *E* trustee and provides that the trustee is required to give Grantor as much income as is needed each year for Grantor's support and maintenance, with any excess income to go to *X*.

(7) Decedent and Spouse each own 10 percent of the voting power of Corporation *A*. Decedent transfers $100,000 to a trust with income to *X* for *X*'s life, and a remainder to *Y* or *Y*'s estate. Decedent is trustee with normal fiduciary powers, including the right to vote stock. Assuming that both spouses each retain their 10 percent ownership, to what extent is Section 2036(a)(1) applicable in the following situations, when Decedent dies survived by Spouse and *X*:

- **(a)** Decedent, as trustee, purchases $100,000 of *A*'s voting common stock (5 percent of the voting stock) from an unrelated third party.
- **(b)** Same as question **(7)(a)**, above, except that Decedent and Spouse each own 7.5 percent of *A*'s voting power.
- **(c)** Same as question **(7)(a)**, above, except the stock is nonvoting stock.
- **(d)** Decedent, as trustee, invests the $100,000, one half in voting stock of *A* (2.5 percent of the total voting stock) and one half in nonvoting stock, again purchased from an unrelated third party.

(8) Schemer is a person not to be outdone by Congress and the Code. Aware of Section 2036, Schemer agrees with Sibling that Schemer will transfer $100,000 in trust, with income to Sibling for Sibling's life, and a remainder to Sibling's children or their estates, if Sibling transfers $100,000 to a trust with income to Schemer for life, and a remainder to Schemer's children or their estates.

- **(a)** What is Schemer trying to do, and will the plan succeed?
- **(b)** What is the result to Schemer if Sibling places only $75,000 in the trust that Sibling creates?

(9) *T* put $100,000 worth of stock in trust with income to *X* (not a dependent) for ten years, and a remainder to *Y* or *Y*'s estate. *T* retained a power to accumulate dividends and add them to corpus. At *T*'s death six years later, the stock was worth $150,000 and the trust had accumulated $25,000 of dividend income.

- **(a)** What is included in *T*'s gross estate under Section 2036?
- **(b)** What is the result in question **(9)(a)**, above, if the remainder had been to *X* or *X*'s estate rather than to *Y* or *Y*'s estate?

(10) Grantor transfers Grantor's principal residence to a trust with income to Grantor for life, and a remainder to Child or Child's estate.

- **(a)** What is included in Grantor's gross estate when, five years prior to death, Grantor sells the income interest, worth $25,000 (based on Grantor's life expectancy and the rental value of the property), to Child for $25,000? At all times, the residence that makes up the corpus of the trust is worth $150,000.
- **(b)** What would be included in Grantor's gross estate if the sale of the income interest in question **(10)(a)**, above (for its then fair market value), was made by Grantor two years prior to Grantor's death?

PROBLEM 5

[*SMLC&S refers to the abridged edition of Federal Estate and Gift Taxation (8th ed.).*]

Assignment

Code:	§§ 2035(a); 2037.
Regulations:	§§ 20.2037-1(a)–20.2037-1(e); 20.7520-3(b)(3)(ii).
SMLC&S:	¶¶ 1.02[2][b][iii]; 4.09[1], 4.09[6].
Suggested references:	Estate of Roy v. Comm'r, 54 TC 1317 (1970).

Questions

(1) Grantor creates a trust with income to Spouse for life, remainder to Child if living and, if not, reversion to Grantor or Grantor's estate.

(a) If Grantor predeceases Spouse and Child, is Section 2037 applicable to the transfer?

(b) Is any part of the value of the trust corpus included in Grantor's gross estate?

(2) Grantor creates a trust with income to *X* or *X*'s estate for Grantor's life, remainder to *Y* if *Y* is then living and, if not, to *Z* or *Z*'s estate. If Grantor predeceases *X* and *Y*, is anything includable in Grantor's gross estate?

(3) What interest or interests, if any, are included in Grantor's gross estate under Section 2037 (assuming the 5 percent test is met) in the following situations:

(a) Grantor creates a trust with income to Spouse, *S*, for life, reversion to Grantor if living and, if not, to *A* or *A*'s estate. Grantor predeceases *S* and *A*.

(b) What is the result if Grantor gave the reversion to *A* and died within two years of the gift?

(c) Grantor creates a trust with income to *S* for life, remainder to *A* if living and, if *A* is not living, reversion to Grantor if Grantor is living; if Grantor is not living, remainder to *B* or *B*'s estate. Grantor predeceases *S* and *A*.

(d) Same as question **(3)(c)**, above, except that *S* is also given a general power of appointment over the property.

(e) Grantor, age 50, creates a trust with income to be accumulated for twenty years or until Grantor's death, whichever is earlier, then principal and accumulated income to Child if living. Grantor dies ten years later, survived by Child. Assume that if Child were not living, principles of local law would effect a reversion to Grantor's estate.

(f) Same as question **(3)(e)**, above, except that Grantor is age 90 at the time of the transfer.

(g) Grantor creates a trust with income to *S* for Grantor's life, with the remainder to *X* or *Y* or their estates in any portions Grantor determines; if Grantor fails to allocate the remainder, it is to pass equally to *X* and *Y* or their estates. Grantor predeceases all parties without allocating the remainder.

(h) Grantor creates a trust with income to *S* for *S*'s life, then income to Grantor for Grantor's life, and a remainder to Children or their estates.

PROBLEM 6

[*SMLC&S refers to the abridged edition of Federal Estate and Gift Taxation (8th ed.).*]

Assignment

Code:	§§ 2035(a), 2035(e); 2038.
Regulations:	§§ 20.2038-1(a), 20.2038-1(b), 20.2038-1(e).
SMLC&S:	¶¶ 4.07[2][b][ii]; 4.10 (omit ¶ 4.10[10]).
Suggested references:	Jennings v. Smith, 161 F2d 74 (2d Cir. 1947), 47-1 USTC ¶ 10,551, 35 AFTR 1203.
	Old Colony Trust Co. v. United States, 423 F2d 601 (1st Cir. 1970), 70-1 USTC ¶ 12,667, 25 AFTR2d 1549.
	Rev. Rul. 70-513, 1970-2 CB 194.

Questions

(1) Grantor creates a trust with income to *X* or *X*'s estate *for Grantor's life*, and a remainder to *Y* or *Y*'s estate. What is the result for Grantor under Section 2038 when Grantor predeceases all other parties in the following situations? This problem is similar to question **(6)** in Problem 4, relating to Section 2036. Consider the results under Section 2036, as well as Section 2038.

- **(a)** Grantor, as trustee, retains a power to invade corpus for *Z*.
- **(b)** Grantor, as trustee, retains a power to give the remainder to *Z*.
- **(c)** Grantor, as trustee, retains a power to invade the corpus of the trust for *X*.
- **(d)** Grantor provides that the trustee shall have power to give corpus to *Z* and names friend *E* trustee.
- **(e)** Grantor creates the trust in question **(1)(d)**, above, but Grantor retains a power to remove *E* as trustee at any time and name Grantor as trustee.

(f) Grantor creates the trust in question **(1)(d)**, above, but Grantor names a corporate trustee and retains the right to remove the trustee without cause and to appoint another corporate trustee.

(g) Grantor names Grantor trustee, and, as the trustee, Grantor is required to give unrelated *Z* as much income as is needed each year for *Z*'s support and maintenance, with any excess income to go to *X*. What results if *Z* is Grantor's minor child?

(h) Grantor retains a power to order the third-party trustee to return all of the trust corpus to Grantor.

(i) Grantor retains the power in question **(1)(h)**, above, but provides that it shall not become effective until six months after Grantor's notice that Grantor intends to exercise it.

(j) Grantor names *X* trustee and retains a power in conjunction with *X* to direct that all of the trust corpus be returned to Grantor.

(k) Grantor retains a power subject to *X*'s and *Y*'s approval to require the third-party trustee to return the trust corpus to Grantor.

(2) Grantor creates a trust with income to *X* (not a dependent) for ten years, and a remainder to *X* or *X*'s estate. Grantor dies after five years, *X* surviving.

(a) What inclusion would be required under Sections 2036 and 2038 if Grantor retained a power to accumulate income?

(b) What inclusion would be required under Sections 2036 and 2038 if Grantor retained a power to invade corpus for *X*?

(3) Settlor transfers some IBM stock to a trust and provides for the payment of income to *A* for *A*'s life, and a remainder to *B* or *B*'s estate. Settlor is trustee and, as trustee, holds the power to vote the stock, to sell the stock and reinvest in other stock, even if it is speculative or unproductive of income, and to allocate receipts other than cash dividends either to income or to principal. What are the estate tax consequences upon the death of Settlor under Sections 2036(a)(2) and 2038?

(4) Grantor makes an inter vivos outright gift of some rental property to Grantor's Spouse. Spouse dies and devises the rental property to a trust that provides income to whichever of their Children the trustee decides for Children's lives, and a remainder to Grandchildren. The trustee may also invade the corpus for any of the Children. Spouse names Grantor as trustee of the trust. Grantor predeceases all of the beneficiaries. What are the estate tax consequences to Grantor?

(5) Grantor created a revocable trust several years ago providing for income to Children and a remainder to Grandchildren. Within three years of Grantor's death, Grantor relinquished the power to revoke the trust.

(a) Is the corpus of the trust included in Grantor's gross estate?

(b) What is the result if, instead, the trust provided income to Grantor for life and a remainder to Children and Grantor relinquished both the income interest and the power to revoke the trust within three years of Grantor's death?

(6) Having studied Sections 2035–2038, and assuming your Client wants to transfer assets to a trust whose corpus will not be included in Client's gross estate, what suggestions do you have for Client to avoid Sections 2035–2038 inclusion in Client's gross estate?

PROBLEM 7

[*SMLC&S refers to the abridged edition of Federal Estate and Gift Taxation (8th ed.).*]

Assignment

Code:	§ 2039. Skim §§ 72(b)(2), 72(b)(3); 2035; 2505.
Regulations:	§§ 20.2039-1(a), 20.2039-1(b)(1), 20.2039-1(c).
SMLC&S:	¶ 4.11 (omit ¶¶ 4.11[2], 4.11[7]).
Suggested references:	All v. McCobb, 321 F2d 633 (2d Cir. 1963), 63-2 USTC ¶ 12,173, 12 AFTR2d 6250. Estate of Bergan v. Comm'r, 1 TC 543 (1943), acq. 1943 CB 2.

Questions

(1) In year 1, *D* entered into a contract with an insurance company under which *D* paid the company $750,000 then and there; they agreed that beginning in year 10, the company would pay *D* $9,000 per month for life and, after *D*'s death, the company would make like payments to *D*'s spouse *S* for as long as *S* should live. However, *D* died in year 8, survived by *S*.

- **(a)** Apply Section 2039 to the facts above.
- **(b)** What is the result in question **(1)(a)**, above, if *S* had paid $250,000 of *S*'s funds toward the $750,000 cost of the contract?
- **(c)** What is the result in question **(1)(a)**, above, if $375,000 of the cost had been paid by *D*'s employer?
- **(d)** Would the results in question **(1)(a)**, above, be different if, pursuant to a "qualified" pension plan, *D*'s employer had purchased the contract for *D* and *S*?
- **(e)** What is *S*'s income tax basis in the right to receive the future payment in question **(1)(d)**, above? If *D* intended to make charitable donations at death, should *D* consider leaving other property to *S* and the pension proceeds to charity?

(2) In year 1, *D* "sold" *D*'s ranch to Child *C*. As full consideration for the transfer, *C* agreed to pay *D* $10,000 per month for *D*'s life, all obligations to cease upon *D*'s death. For several years, the net income from the ranch had been approximately $10,000 per month. *D* died in year 5, the current year.

- **(a)** If the value of the ranch equals the value of *C*'s agreement to pay, of what estate tax significance is this arrangement upon *D*'s death?
- **(b)** Would the result be different if the agreement called for $10,000 payments each month to *D* for *D*'s life and thereafter to *D*'s spouse for spouse's life if spouse should survive *D*? (*D*'s spouse survives.)
- **(c)** Assuming only payments to *D* and assuming that the ranch was worth $2 million and the value of *C*'s agreement to pay was $1 million, what are the estate tax consequences at *D*'s death?Consider generally whether the gift tax makes the conclusion acceptable.
- **(d)** If, at the time of transfer, the ranch was worth $2 million and the agreement to pay was worth $1 million, and *D* died in year 2 at a time when the ranch was worth $2.5 million, what are the consequences to *D*'s estate?
- **(e)** The arrangement in question **(2)(a)**, above, is a "sale," a transfer for adequate and full consideration, although if *D* outlives *D*'s life expectancy, it can be expensive for *C*. What alternative "sale" estate planning techniques are available to *D*?

There are also important income tax consequences to private arrangements in the form of property transfers in exchange for annuities. See IRC § 72(b)(2); Rev. Rul. 69-74, 1969-1 CB 43 (consequences to transferor); Rev. Rul. 55-119, 1955-1 CB 352 (consequences to transferee). But see Prop. Reg. §§ 1.72-6(e), 1.1001-1(j).

PROBLEM 8

[SMLC&S refers to the abridged edition of Federal Estate and Gift Taxation (8th ed.).]

Assignment

Code:	§§ 2040; 2056(d)(1)(B).
Regulations:	§ 20.2040-1.
SMLC&S:	¶ 4.12 (omit ¶ 4.12[11]).
Suggested references:	Estate of Peters v. Comm'r, 386 F2d 404 (4th Cir. 1967), 67-2 USTC ¶ 12,497, 20 AFTR2d 6016.
	Gallenstein v. United States, 975 F2d 286 (6th Cir. 1992), 92-2 USTC ¶ 60,114, 70 AFTR2d 5683.
	Tuck v. United States, 282 F2d 405 (9th Cir. 1960), 60-2 USTC ¶ 11,968, 6 AFTR2d 6150.
	United States v. Heasty, 370 F2d 525 (10th Cir. 1966), 67-1 USTC ¶ 12,442, 19 AFTR2d 1767.

Questions

(1) Consider the estate taxation of property owned by the decedent and another.

- **(a)** How does the Code deal with Community property?
- **(b)** How does the Code deal with a tenancy in common?
- **(c)** How does the Code deal with a joint tenancy with right of survivorship?
- **(d)** How does the Code deal with a tenancy by the entirety?
- **(e)** Are there good policy reasons (and what are the reasons) for according different estate tax treatment to property owned by the decedent and another in various forms of joint ownership?
- **(f)** How does the Code deal with the estate taxation of property held in a revocable trust funded by the decedent? Are the consequences comparable to ownership with a right of survivorship?

(2) Child contributed $5,000 of Child's funds to a joint savings account between Parent and Child. Upon Parent's death several years later, $20,000 was in the account. The origin of $15,000 of the $20,000 is obscure, but there had been no withdrawals. How does the savings account affect Parent's gross estate when Parent predeceases Child? See Estate of Drazen v. Comm'r, 48 TC 1 (1967).

(3) A parcel of joint tenancy real property owned by Parent and Child was worth $25,000 at its acquisition in 1995 and $50,000 at decedent's death. What is the result under Section 2040 in the following situations?

- **(a)** Parent paid the full $25,000 purchase price; Parent predeceases Child.
- **(b)** Parent paid the full $25,000 purchase price; Child predeceases Parent.
- **(c)** Parent and Child each contributed $12,500 of the purchase price; Parent predeceases Child.
- **(d)** Parent contributed $15,000 of the purchase price and Child contributed $10,000; Parent predeceases Child.
- **(e)** Grandparent devised the property to Parent and Child as joint tenants; Parent predeceases Child.
- **(f)** What would the results be in questions **(3)(a)**, **(3)(b)**, and **(3)(d)**, above, if the joint tenants were spouses, not Parent and Child?

(4) Discuss the estate tax consequences of the following transactions in joint tenancy property under Section 2040:

- **(a)** Parent transfers stock outright to Child, who subsequently transfers the same stock, which has not appreciated, to Parent and Child as joint tenants. At the time of Child's transfer, the stock is worth $5,000. Parent predeceases Child when the stock is worth $10,000.
- **(b)** Same as question **(4)(a)**, above, except that in the current year, Child predeceases Parent within three years of Child's transfer. The stock is worth $10,000 at Child's death.
- **(c)** Parent transfers stock outright to Child. Child subsequently uses ordinary cash dividends paid on the stock to pay the entire purchase price for the stock in a joint tenancy between Parent and Child. Parent predeceases Child when the jointly owned stock is worth $10,000.

(d) Parent transfers stock worth $5,000 outright to Child. When the stock has appreciated in value to $10,000, Child sells it and uses the proceeds to purchase other stock worth $10,000 in joint tenancy between Parent and Child. Parent predeceases Child when the jointly owned stock is worth $20,000.

(e) Same as question **(4)(d)**, above, except that rather than selling the original stock, Child transfers it when it is worth $10,000 to a joint tenancy between Parent and Child.

(5) Parent purchased a piece of commercial property for $40,000 to which Parent and Child took title as joint tenants. Several years later, when the property had appreciated in value to $50,000, Parent and Child made a $25,000 improvement to the property (increasing its value to $75,000), with Child providing $15,000 and Parent providing $10,000 of the cost of the improvement. Parent predeceased Child several years later when the property was worth $125,000. What is included in Parent's gross estate under Section 2040?

(6) Grandparent purchased some land in the current year for $20,000 and contributed it to a joint tenancy with Child. Five years later, Grandparent became terminally ill and several weeks before Grandparent's death, Grandparent and Child severed the joint tenancy property, then worth $50,000, and converted it to a tenancy-in-common.

(a) What is the result for Grandparent's gross estate when Grandparent dies with Child surviving?

(b) What is the result for Child's gross estate when Child dies with Grandparent surviving and the property worth $50,000?

(c) What are the results in questions **(6)(a)** and **(6)(b)**, above, if, rather than converting the property to a tenancy-in-common, Grandparent and Child transfer it retaining a joint life tenancy?

(7) **Community Property Question**: Recently married clients who live in a community property state ask your advice on whether they should take title to their newly acquired residence as joint tenants or as community property. What do you advise?

PROBLEM 9

[SMLC&S refers to the abridged edition of Federal Estate and Gift Taxation (8th ed.). Appendix begins on page 103 of the Study Problems.]

Assignment

Code:	§§ 2041(a)(1), 2041(a)(2), 2041(b); 2046. Skim § 2518.
Regulations:	§§ 20.2041-1(a)–20.2041-1(c)(2), 20.2041-1(e); 20.2041-3(a)–20.2041-3(d)(1).
SCLC&S:	¶¶ 4.13 (omit ¶¶ 4.13[8][b], 4.13[10]); 4.18; 10.07[1].
Appendix:	Applicable Credit Amount Table.
Suggested references:	Fish v. United States, 432 F2d 1278 (9th Cir. 1970), 70-2 USTC ¶ 12,718, 26 AFTR2d 6070. Keeter v. United States, 461 F2d 714 (5th Cir. 1972), 72-1 USTC ¶ 12,839, 29 AFTR2d 1540.

Questions

(1) Indicate the extent to which *D* has a general power of appointment, if at all, in the following circumstances:

- **(a)** *D* has the right to appoint any or all of the corpus of a trust created by *D*'s sibling *S* to anyone other than *D*'s brother *B*.
- **(b)** Same as question **(1)(a)**, above, except that *D* can exercise *D*'s power, which was created after 1942, only with the consent of *B*, who has no interest in the trust. Why is the date of creation of the power important here?
- **(c)** Same as question **(1)(a)**, above, except that *D* can exercise *D*'s power only with *S*'s consent.
- **(d)** Same as question **(1)(a)**, above, except that *D*'s power, created after 1942, can be exercised only with the consent of *Y*, who, after *D*'s death, will alone have the power to appoint the trust corpus to anyone.

(e) Same as question **(1)(a)**, above, except that *D*'s power, created after 1942, can be exercised only with the consent of *Z*, to whom the property may also be appointed, but who will have no power over the trust after the death of *D*.

(2) By a will effective upon *X*'s death in 1940, *X* created a trust under which *D* had the right to the income for life.

(a) In addition, at *D*'s death, *D* had the power to appoint the property to or among the descendants of *X*. In default of *D*'s appointment, the remainder went to *R* or *R*'s estate. *D* died in the current year, validly appointing the property by will to *X*'s grandchild *G*. Is the property includable in *D*'s gross estate? Are we assuming something in our answer here?

(b) Would your answer in question **(2)(a)**, above, be different if, while the property was appointed to *G*, *D* also had the power to direct the use of the property at *D*'s death to pay claims against *D*'s estate?

(c) What is the result under the facts of question **(2)(b)**, above, if, even though *D* had the additional power just mentioned, *D* executed no will and at *D*'s death the property passed to *R*?

(d) What is the result in question **(2)(b)**, above, if *D* had the additional power to direct the use of the property to pay claims against *D*'s estate, but only if *Y*, who had been *X*'s spouse, approved of such use of the funds?

(3) Consider the following circumstances with regard to possible estate tax liability upon the death of *D*, assuming that any powers in *D* were created under the will of *X*, who died in 1990.

(a) *D*, life income beneficiary of a trust created by *X*, had a power to appoint the trust corpus to anyone, but died in the current year without ever exercising the power. Upon default of *D*'s appointment, the property passed to *Y* or *Y*'s estate.

(b) How might *D* have averted any estate or gift tax consequences in question **(3)(a)**, above? What should *D* have done and when?

(c) Same as question **(3)(a)**, above, except that *D* could not exercise *D*'s power until six months after written notice to the remainder person *R* that *D* intended to do so, and *D* died in the current year without ever having given such notice.

(d) Same as question **(3)(a)**, above, except that *D*'s power was not exercisable until after the death of *R*, and *D* died in the current year survived by *R*.

PROBLEM 9

(4) *A* held a general power to appoint by deed only. It had been created after 1942, and *A* died without exercising it. What are the estate tax consequences to *A*?

(5) Decedent was the income beneficiary of a trust created by Grantor with a remainder to *Z* or *Z*'s estate. Decedent also had a noncumulative general power to appoint $10,000 per year out of the corpus of the trust, which at all times had a value of $200,000. The trust was created five years ago, and each year, by reason of nonexercise, the noncumulative general power to appoint lapsed.

- **(a)** What are the estate tax consequences to Decedent's estate upon Decedent's death exactly five years after creation of the trust?
- **(b)** What is the result if Decedent was given the noncumulative power to appoint the $10,000 only in January of each year and Decedent died in a month other than January in year 5?
- **(c)** What is the result in question **(5)(a)**, above, if Decedent's noncumulative power to appoint was $15,000 per year rather than $10,000? See Reg. § 20.2041-3(d)(3).
- **(d)** What is the result in question **(5)(c)**, above, if the trust corpus appreciated from $200,000 to $300,000 in the year of Decedent's death? See Reg. § 20.2041-3(d)(4).

(6) Wealthy, who is unmarried with no children, has one younger Sibling, who is married with several children. Sibling's assets are worth approximately $4 million. Wealthy's assets are worth approximately $2 million. Wealthy wishes to provide for Sibling and Sibling's family to the maximum extent possible, but not to burden Sibling's estate with "unnecessary" estate taxes. What do you advise?

PROBLEM 10

[*SMLC&S refers to the abridged edition of Federal Estate and Gift Taxation (8th ed.).*]

Assignment

Code:	§ 2042. Skim § 2035(a).
Regulations:	§§ 20.2031-8(a); 20.2042-1.
SMLC&S:	¶ 4.14 (omit ¶¶ 4.14[2][b], 4.14[10]).
Suggested references:	Estate of Headrick v. Comm'r, 918 F2d 1263 (6th Cir. 1990), 90-2 USTC ¶ 60,049, 66 AFTR2d 6038. Estate of Levy v. Comm'r, 70 TC 873 (1978). Rev. Rul. 84-179, 1984-2 CB 195.

Questions

(1) *X* took out a $10,000 single-premium insurance policy on *X*'s life and immediately assigned all right, title, and interest in the policy to *D*. *D* died one year later, survived by *X*. Is anything includable in *D*'s gross estate with respect to the policy? Why?

(2) *D* took out an insurance policy on *D*'s life, primarily to ensure the availability of cash for payment of claims and taxes when *D* died.

(a) The policy was payable to *D*'s bank to pay for the mortgage on *D*'s residence. Is it includable?

(b) The policy permits *D* to change the beneficiary. If *D* now makes *D*'s spouse, *S*, the beneficiary, will the policy escape inclusion in *D*'s gross estate on *D*'s death?

(c) What must also be considered by *D* if *D*'s objective is exclusion from *D*'s gross estate?

(3) Insured takes out a life insurance policy on Insured's life, and, more than three years prior to Insured's death, the following events occur. To what extent are the life insurance proceeds included in Insured's gross estate at Insured's death?

(a) Insured transfers the policy to Spouse. Spouse predeceases Insured and transfers Spouse's residuary estate, including the life insurance policy, to a trust naming Insured as trustee. Under the terms of the trust, income is to be paid to *A* for *A*'s life, with a remainder to *B* or *B*'s estate. Insured, as trustee, has the power to surrender the policy and receive its cash surrender value as a trust asset and to invade the trust corpus for the benefit of *A* or *A*'s estate.

(b) Same as question **(3)(a)**, above, except that Insured may invade the trust corpus for Insured's own benefit rather than for *A* or *A*'s estate's benefit.

(c) Insured transfers the policy to a trust providing for income to *A* for *A*'s life, with a remainder to *B* or *B*'s estate. Insured is trustee with normal fiduciary powers, including the power to surrender the policy and receive the cash surrender value of the policy as a trust asset.

(4) Insured owned 60 percent of the voting stock of Corporation, which owned a policy on Insured's life. The minority 40 percent shareholder was beneficiary of the policy, but Corporation held the incidents of ownership in the policy.

(a) To what extent are the proceeds of the policy included in Insured's gross estate at Insured's death?

(b) To what extent are the proceeds includable if Corporation is the beneficiary of the policy?

(5) Taxpayer had an insurance policy on Taxpayer's life on which Taxpayer had paid premiums for ten years. The proceeds of the policy are $200,000 and are to be paid to Sibling on Taxpayer's death. In the tenth year, Taxpayer conveyed the policy to Sibling, but, unless stated to the contrary, Taxpayer continued to pay the premiums. Taxpayer did not, however, retain "any incidents of ownership."

(a) What are the estate tax consequences if Taxpayer dies two years after conveyance?

(b) What are the estate tax consequences if Taxpayer dies two years after conveyance, but Sibling has paid the post-transfer premiums?

(c) What are the estate tax consequences if Taxpayer dies four years after conveyance?

(d) What are the estate tax consequences if Taxpayer dies four years after conveyance, but Sibling has paid the post-transfer premiums?

(e) What are the estate tax consequences if Sibling took out the policy on Taxpayer's life two years prior to Taxpayer's death, but Taxpayer paid all of the premiums on the policy?

(6) Insured transferred an insurance policy on Insured's life along with other property to a revocable trust four years ago. One year prior to Insured's accidental death, Insured relinquished the right to revoke the trust. To what extent is the corpus of the trust included in Insured's gross estate?

(7) **Community Property Question**: Spouses use community property funds to purchase a policy on Insured Spouse's life over which Insured Spouse holds the incidents of ownership.

- **(a)** What are the tax consequences at Insured Spouse's death, Non-Insured Spouse surviving, if the proceeds are paid to Child?
- **(b)** Same as question **(7)(a)**, above, except what are the tax consequences if the proceeds are paid to Insured Spouse's estate?
- **(c)** What are the tax consequences at Non-Insured Spouse's death if Non-Insured Spouse predeceases Insured Spouse?

PROBLEM 11

[SMLC&S refers to the abridged edition of Federal Estate and Gift Taxation (8th ed.). Appendix begins on page 103 of the Study Problems.]

Assignment

Code:	§§ 2031 (omit § 2031(c)); 2032(a), 2032(c), 2032(d); 2032A(a), 2032A(b), 2032A(c)(1)–2032A(c)(5), 2032A(e)(1), 2032A(e)(2), 2032A(e)(7), 2032A(e)(8); 2703. Skim the remainder of §§ 2032A; 1014(a), 1014(c); 1016(c); 6662; 7517; 7520.
Regulations:	§§ 20.2031-1(b); 20.2032-1; 20.6151-1(c); 25.2703-1(a), 25.2703-1(b).
SMLC&S:	¶¶ 1.02[2][c]; 4.02[2], 4.02[3][f], 4.02[4]; 4.03[1], 4.03[3]; 4.04[1], 4.04[2], 4.04[7][a]; 19.04 (skim ¶¶ 19.04[3][a], 19.04[3][c]; omit ¶¶ 19.04[6][b], 19.04[6][c]).
Appendix:	Table S.
Suggested references:	Estate of Amile, 91 TCM (CCH) 1017 (2006).
	Estate of Hance v. Comm'r, 18 TC 499 (1952), acq. 1953-1 CB 4.
	Estate of Seltzer v. Comm'r, 50 TCM (CCH) 1250 (1985).
	Estate of Strangi v. Comm'r, 417 F3d 468 (5th Cir. 2005).
	Kimbell v. United States, 371 F3d 257 (5th Cir. 2004).

Questions

(1) Decedent held stock in a close corporation. The fair market value of Decedent's stock on the open market at Decedent's death, without regard to any agreements, was $2 million and its book value was $1,500,000. Under an agreement, during Decedent's life the corporation had a right of first refusal if Decedent elected to sell Decedent's stock. In addition, at Decedent's death the corporation had a "call option" under which the corporation could elect to purchase the stock for its book value.

(a) If Decedent is the sole shareholder of the corporation, what value does the stock have in Decedent's gross estate?

(b) If Decedent owns one third of the stock of the corporation, Decedent's siblings own the other two thirds, and the siblings' stock is subject to the same agreement, what value does the stock have in Decedent's gross estate?

(c) If Decedent owns one third of the stock of the corporation, unrelated persons own the other two thirds, and the unrelated persons' stock is subject to the same agreement, what value does the stock have in Decedent's gross estate?

(2) Decedent's family owned a partnership that invested in real estate that was worth $4 million at Decedent's death. Decedent owns a one-quarter interest in the family partnership.

(a) What is the value of Decedent's partnership interest for estate tax purposes?

(b) If Decedent's interest qualifies for a 20 percent minority discount and a 20 percent marketability discount, what is the value of Decedent's partnership interest for estate tax purposes?

(c) Is there any difference in result in question **(2)(b)**, above, if Decedent had given away another 40 percent interest in the partnership two years prior to Decedent's death?

(d) What is the result in question **(2)(b)**, above, if the real estate was in a corporation rather than a partnership?

(3) Parent, (*P*), and *P*'s two children, (*D*) and (*S*), formed corporation, (*C*). *P*, *D*, and *S* each contributed cash to *C* and received an amount of *C* stock proportionate to their contributions. *P* received 40 percent of the *C* stock, and *D* and *S* each received 30 percent of *C* stock. *P* and *C* formed a family limited partnership, *FLP*. *P* retained his residences and a sufficient stock and bond portfolio to provide income for *P*'s support and maintenance and to make annual gifts, but *P* transferred *P*'s remaining stock and bond portfolio to *FLP* and received a 99 percent limited partnership interest in return for the transfer. *C* transferred cash to *FLP* for a one percent general partnership interest in *FLP*. The assets transferred to *FLP* directly or indirectly by *P* were worth $10 million when *P* died one year later. *P*'s personal representative included *P*'s 99 percent limited partnership interest and *P*'s *C* stock worth 40 percent of the one percent general partnership interest in *P*'s gross estate under Section

2033. *P*'s personal representative took discounts that resulted in a 40 percent reduction and included only $6 million in *P*'s gross estate. Consider the proper amount that should be included in *P*'s gross estate.

(4) In year 1, *X* bequeathed certain securities to a trust, the income to be paid to *B* for life and, upon *B*'s death, the remainder to go to *D* or *D*'s estate. At the time of *D*'s death in year 10, survived by *B*, the securities were worth $100,000 and *B* was age 70. Six months later, the securities had doubled in value to $200,000 and *B* was then age 71. (Although *B* would be only six months older, use annual actuarial figures for simplicity.) Using Table S, located in the Appendix, and assuming a 6 percent interest rate, what should be included in *D*'s gross estate with respect to the trust property if:

(a) *D*'s executor values the estate as of *D*'s death?
(b) *D*'s executor values the estate as of the alternate valuation date?
(c) *B* dies within six months following *D*'s death and *D*'s executor elects the alternate valuation date?
(d) Three months after *D*'s death, the securities are sold and the proceeds are reinvested at a time when the securities are worth $150,000 and executor elects the alternate valuation date?

(5) Decedent, who died in the current year, owned a farm with a fair market value of $6 million. The farm was the only real property in the estate, and it constituted the major portion of the estate. Assume that the farm qualifies for valuation under Section 2032A and, under the formula farm valuation method, its valuation is $4 million. The farm is devised to Child, who agrees to a Section 2032A election.

(a) How much of the value of the farm will be included in Decedent's gross estate?
(b) What is the income tax basis of the farm after the 2032A election? See IRC § 1014.
(c) What are the additional estate tax consequences if Child sells the farm to an unrelated third person for $7 million five years after Decedent's death?
(d) Who bears the tax liability for the additional estate tax?
(e) Would it make any difference if, instead of a farm, Decedent's sole asset was an office building used in a trade or business?

PROBLEM 12

[*SMLC&S refers to the abridged edition of Federal Estate and Gift Taxation (8th ed.).*]

Assignment

Code: §§ 642(g); 2043(b); 2051; 2053 (omit § 2053(d)); 2054. Skim §§ 163(k); 213(c); 641(b); 691(b); 2516.

Regulations: §§ 1.642(g); 20.2032-1(g); 20.2053-1, 20.2053-3, 20.2053-4, 20.2053-7, 20.2053-8(a); 20.2054-1.

SMLC&S: ¶¶ 5.01; 5.02; 5.03 (skim ¶¶ 5.03[4], 5.03[7]; omit ¶¶ 5.03[8]). Skim ¶ 5.04.

Suggested references: Propstra v. United States, 680 F2d 1248 (9th Cir. 1982), 82-2 USTC ¶ 13,475, 50 AFTR2d 6153.

Questions

(1) *D* died in the current year. The executor of *D*'s estate did not want to sell stock of *D*'s closely held corporation to pay federal estate taxes because the executor did not want the estate to lose control of the corporation.

Yes Administrative Expense

(a) *D*'s executor took out a bank loan to pay estate taxes. Is the interest on the loan deductible under Section 2053?

(b) *D*'s estate qualified under Section 6166 to defer payment of taxes attributable to the value of *D*'s stock in the corporation. Is Section 6601 interest on the estate tax obligation deductible under Section 2053? NO 2053(c)(1)(D)

(2) Ten years ago, *D* transferred *D*'s assets to a revocable trust under an instrument that provided that the trustee was to pay the income to *D* for *D*'s life and, at *D*'s death, to pay the corpus to child *C* or *C*'s estate. When *D* died in the current year, the trust corpus had substantial value, and the trustee charged a reasonable termination commission of $10,000 in connection with the distribution of the assets to *C*.

(a) Does it seem that the $10,000 payment should qualify as an estate tax deduction?

(b) Is there an obstacle to its deductibility under Section 2053(a)?
(c) What is the congressional answer?

(3) Are the following expenses deductible under Section 2053?

(a) Attorney fees paid to probate Decedent's estate.
(b) Trustee fees in administering Decedent's revocable trust (that terminated at Decedent's death) during the period between the date of death and the winding up of the affairs of the trust.
(c) A bequest to Attorney from Decedent.
(d) Personal Representative's fees of $50,000 incurred in probating Decedent's estate in the current year. Assume Decedent made no taxable gifts and Decedent's taxable estate considering all deductions other than fees is $3,525,000. What would you advise Personal Representative to do?

(4) While living, Schemer promised Spouse that if Spouse would be kind and loving, Schemer would leave Spouse $400,000 of Schemer's $1 million estate; but Schemer didn't.

(a) Is Spouse's claim against Schemer's estate deductible under Section 2053?
(b) What is the result if Schemer's promise was made in a separation agreement with Spouse, and was a promise, binding on Schemer's estate and becoming effective upon Schemer's death, to pay Spouse $10,000 a year until Spouse died or remarried for a relinquishment of Spouse's rights to support?
(c) What is the result in question **(4)(b)**, above, if Spouse remarried on the day of Schemer's funeral, a few days after Schemer's death? Would that affect the amount of the deduction?

(5) *D* seriously injured *X* in an accident that caused *D*'s death. Is *X*'s claim against *D*'s estate deductible? If there is uncertainty as to whether the estate is liable, how does that affect the deduction?

(6) Decedent, a cash-method taxpayer, has a principal residence upon which Decedent has a mortgage with $5,000 of accrued interest at the time of Decedent's death. Decedent's personal representative pays the accrued interest and also pays $1,000 a month in interest on the mortgage during the administration of the estate. Discuss the deductibility of the $5,000 accrued interest payment and the $1,000 monthly interest payments.

(7) When *D* died, *D* had only $50,000 in a bank account and no other assets. However, this is the same *D* encountered in question **(2)**, above, and *D* had been receiving $90,000 income annually from the trust, the corpus of which had a value of $1,400,000 at *D*'s death. *D* was personally liable for obligations in the amount of $100,000 when *D* died. This is, therefore, a taxable estate. Could Congress properly take the position that the deduction for claims should not exceed $50,000, since that is all *D* had from which claims can be paid, and that it is of no estate tax significance if *C* pays $50,000 of *D*'s claims from *C*'s own separate funds? What has Congress done about this?

(8) *D*, in the current year, owned a piece of rental residential property that was worth $100,000 at *D*'s death. As a result of a fire, which occurred one month after *D*'s death, the value of the property declined to only $25,000, which was also its value on the alternate valuation date.

- **(a)** If the estate pays death taxes on the basis of date-of-death value, may it claim both an income tax deduction for the loss under Section 165 and an estate tax casualty loss deduction under Section 2054?
- **(b)** If the estate elects the alternate valuation date, will a Section 2054 deduction or a Section 165 deduction be allowed?

PROBLEM 13

[SMLC&S refers to the abridged edition of Federal Estate and Gift Taxation (8th ed.).]

Assignment

Code: §§ 170(f)(3); 642(c)(5); 664(d), 664(e); 2031(c); 2032(b); 2055 (omit § 2055(e)(1), 2055(e)(3), 2055(f), 2055(g)). Skim § 2518.

SMLC&S: ¶¶ 4.02[7]; 5.05 (skim ¶¶ 5.05[1][b], 5.05[3][b], 5.05[5]–5.05[7]; omit ¶¶ 5.05[1][c], 5.05[8]).

Suggested references: Estate of Blackford, 77 TC 1246 (1981), acq. 1983-2 CB 1.

S. Rep. No. 552, 91st Cong., 2d Sess. (1969), reprinted in 1969-3 CB 423, 479–483.

Questions

(1) Decedent left property to a trust generally qualified as a charitable remainder annuity trust as defined in Section 664(d)(1), with provision for suitable fixed annual payments to *A* for *A*'s life, and a remainder to a charity described in Section 2055(a). However, in addition, Decedent provided that *A* could invade the corpus of the trust for *A*'s happiness anytime during *A*'s life. *A* died three months after Decedent's death.

- **(a)** Assuming that *A* did not exercise *A*'s power, to what extent, if at all, will the next to the last sentence of Section 2055(a) ensure a charitable deduction for Decedent's estate?
- **(b)** Consider the estate tax consequences to *A*'s estate.
- **(c)** Now assume *A* was given no power to invade and Decedent placed all the assets in Decedent's gross estate in the trust. If the estate otherwise qualifies for a Section 2032 election, will the amount of the charitable deduction reflect the fact that *A* has died?

(2) *D* dies in the current year, leaving specified shares of stock to a testamentary trust, with income to *A* for *A*'s life, and a remainder to a charity described in Section 2055(a)(2).

(a) Is *D*'s estate entitled to a Section 2055 deduction?

(b) What is the result in question **(2)(a)**, above, if, in lieu of income distributions, *D* provides that *A* will receive an amount equal to 6 percent of the original fair market value of the trust each year of *A*'s life, with a remainder to charity that is valued at more than 10 percent of the value of the property placed in the trust?

(c) What is the result in question **(2)(b)**, above, if *A* is to receive $4,000 per year from the trust and the fair market value of the original trust property was $ 100,000?

(d) What is the result in question **(2)(a)**, above, if *D* provides that each year *A* will receive 6 percent of the fair market value of the trust corpus determined on an annual basis and the remainder is valued at more than 10 percent of the value of the property placed in the trust?

(e) What is the result in question **(2)(d)**, above, if, in addition, *D* provides that if the actual trust income is less than the 6 percent amount, the trustee is required to distribute only the actual trust income to *A*, but if such a deficit occurs, it shall be made up in subsequent years by the excess of actual trust income over the 6 percent amount?

(3) By will, Decedent creates a trust with income to University Law School for twenty years, remainder to Child.

(a) Will Decedent's estate be allowed a Section 2055 deduction?

(b) Will Decedent's estate be allowed a Section 2055 deduction if, in lieu of annual income payments, Decedent requires that $6,000 be paid annually to Law School from the trust, and the trust corpus at the time of creation of the trust is $100,000?

(c) Will Decedent's estate be allowed a Section 2055 deduction if, in lieu of the annual income payments, Decedent requires that 4 percent of the value of the corpus (determined annually) be paid annually to Law School from the trust?

(4) *D* decides to leave *D*'s personal residence to a qualified charity but to let *D*'s child *C* have the benefit of it first for *C*'s life.

(a) *D* devises the residence directly to *C* for life, remainder to charity. Does the value of the remainder interest qualify for a Section 2055 deduction?

(b) *D* leaves the residence in trust, the income to *C* for life, remainder to charity. Does the value of the remainder interest qualify for a Section 2055 deduction?

(c) What is the result in question **(4)(a)**, above, if the residence was *D*'s summer home and, at *C*'s death, the residence was to be sold and the proceeds distributed equally to two different charities?

(5) Decedent's Executor properly deeds a qualified conservation easement to charity on land included in Decedent's gross estate and takes a Section 2055(f) deduction. Decedent's Executor elects on Decedent's federal estate tax return to exclude a portion of the value of the land subject to the easement under Section 2031(c). The land is not subject to any liability and the easement is not liable for its share of federal estate tax.

(a) If the land is worth $500,000, the qualified conservation easement is worth $200,000 and the year of Decedent's death is the current year, consider the consequences of the deduction and election to Decedent's taxable estate.

(b) Same facts as question **(5)(a)**, above, except the land is worth $1 million.

(c) Would Decedent have been better off taxwise in question **(5)(a)**, above, if Decedent had deeded the conservation easement during Decedent's life?

PROBLEM 14

[SMLC&S refers to the abridged edition of Federal Estate and Gift Taxation (8th ed.). Appendix begins on page 103 of the Study Problems.]

Assignment

Code:	§§ 2044; 2056 (omit § 2056(d)(5)); 2207A. Skim §§ 2010; 2046; 2056A; 2518; 2519.
Regulations:	§§ 20.2056(a)-1(a), 20.2056(a)-1(b); 20.2056(b)-1, 20.2056(b)-5(a), 20.2056(b)-7(a)–20.2056(b)-7(d); 20.2056(c)-1.
SMLC&S:	¶¶ 5.06 (skim ¶¶ 5.06[3], 5.06[5], 5.06[8][b], 5.06[8][c]; omit ¶¶ 5.06[8][d][iv], 5.06[10]); 5.07[1]. Skim ¶¶ 4.16; 8.07 (omit ¶ 8.07[3]).
Appendix:	Applicable Credit Amount Table.
Suggested references:	Estate of Clayton v. Comm'r, 976 F2d 1486 (5th Cir. 1992), 92-2 USTC ¶ 60,121, 70 AFTR2d 6262.
	Jackson v. United States, 376 US 503 (1964), 64-1 USTC ¶ 12,221, 13 AFTR2d 1859.
	Kasper v. Kellar, 217 F2d 744 (8th Cir. 1954), 55-1 USTC ¶ 11,501, 46 AFTR 1387 (see also opinion on remand, 138 F. Supp. 738 (DSD 1956)), 56-1 USTC ¶ 11,602, 49 AFTR 600.
	Rev. Rul. 72-7, 1972-1 CB 308.
	Rev. Rul. 72-333, 1972-2 CB 530.

Questions

(1) In this question and the succeeding questions in this problem (unless the facts indicate to the contrary), assume all parties are U.S. citizens. Your clients, a married couple, come to you for estate-planning advice. Each spouse has assets worth $3 million. They have children, but both wish to provide for the other in preference to their children. Neither spouse has made any taxable inter vivos gifts. What do you advise them to do? See IRC § 2010.

(2) By will, *D* left Blackacre to *A* for life, remainder to *B*. *D*'s residuary estate was left to *S*, *D*'s spouse. Both *A* and *B* effectively, under Section 2518, disclaimed their interests in Blackacre.

- **(a)** How may this affect the marital deduction for *D*'s estate?
- **(b)** Is the answer the same if *C* is the residuary legatee under *D*'s will, but, after *D*'s death, *A* and *B* effectively direct the transfer of Blackacre to *S*?
- **(c)** Under what circumstances (and with what effect) might a surviving spouse be likely to disclaim an interest in property left to the surviving spouse?

(3) Spouses own Blackacre, worth $1 million, as tenants by the entirety. Spouses purchased Blackacre in 1990. Upon the death of one of the spouses:

- **(a)** Does an interest in property pass from Decedent to Surviving Spouse?
- **(b)** What is the amount of the marital deduction?

(4) Decedent leaves property in trust, the income to be paid to Parent for Parent's life and, at Parent's death, the corpus to be distributed to Decedent's Spouse or Spouse's estate. Does the transfer qualify for a marital deduction?

(5) Carefully review the three elements of the terminable interest rule (IRC § 2056(b)(1)); then apply the elements to determine whether the following interests are deductible or nondeductible, assuming in each instance that *S* is *D*'s surviving spouse.

- **(a)** *D* sold property to *D*'s child, *C*, for $50,000, but retained possession for a term of years. The fair market value of the remainder interest transferred to *C* was $50,000. When *D* died, *D* still had the right to possession of the property for ten years, which right *D* left to *S*.
- **(b)** Same as question **(5)(a)**, above, except that *D* made a gift of the remainder interest in the property to *C*, instead of selling it to *C*.
- **(c)** *D*, by a will provision, ordered *D*'s executor to buy a $100,000 single-premium life annuity for *S*.

(6) Decedent by will leaves $500,000 of property to a testamentary trust under which the trustee is to pay any amount of income that trustee deems desirable to Decedent's Surviving Spouse, and any accumulated income and corpus to Surviving Spouse's estate at Surviving Spouse's death. Does the $500,000 qualify for the marital deduction?

(7) *D* dies leaving property outright to *D*'s spouse, *S*, but with an effective provision defeating *S*'s interest and diverting the property to others if *S* "should not live long enough to probate" *D*'s will. If *S* lives until *D*'s will is probated, which occurs within six months of *D*'s death, will the property qualify for the marital deduction?

(8) *D* dies leaving $6 million worth of property in trust. The terms of the trust provide that the income from the trust is to be paid monthly. Determine the marital deduction, if any, in the following circumstances:

- **(a)** The terms of the trust provide for an income interest to Surviving Spouse for life, with a testamentary power to appoint the property to Surviving Spouse's estate and, in default of appointment, to their children.
- **(b)** Surviving Spouse receives an income interest for life, with remainder going to the Children of *D*'s first marriage.
- **(c)** Same as question **(8)(b)**, above, and a Section 2056(b)(7) election was made. What further estate or gift consequences will occur? Consider as well the liability for any tax consequences.
- **(d)** What is the result if the provision is the same as in question **(8)(b)**, above, except that if a Section 2056(b)(7) election is not made to all or any portion of the property held in trust, the unelected property passes to the children outright?
- **(e)** What is the result in question **(8)(b)**, above, if the third-party trustee of the trust has the power to accumulate the income of the trust?
- **(f)** Same as question **(8)(b)**, above, except that Surviving Spouse is given a testamentary nongeneral power to appoint among the Children of *D*'s first marriage.
- **(g)** Same as question **(8)(b)**, above, except that a third-party trustee, not Surviving Spouse, holds the testamentary nongeneral power to appoint among the Children.
- **(h)** Same as question **(8)(b)**, above, except that Surviving Spouse is given an inter vivos power to appoint the corpus of the trust among the Children of *D*'s first marriage.
- **(i)** Same as question **(8)(b)**, above, except that the third-party trustee has a power to invade corpus for the benefit of Surviving Spouse.
- **(j)** Same as question **(8)(i)**, above, and the $6 million was *D*'s total

gross estate. What would you advise *D*'s executor with respect to a Section 2056(b)(7)(B)(v) election?

(k) If there is an election with respect to only some of the property, may *D*'s executor create separate trusts for the elective and nonelective shares? Must the trusts be funded with a proportionate share of each asset in the estate? See Reg. § 20.2056(b)-7(b)(2)(ii).

(9) Decedent leaves $1 million worth of property to a qualified charitable remainder annuity trust with the annuity to go to Surviving Spouse for life.

(a) Will any of the property qualify for the marital deduction?

(b) Rather than using a qualified remainder trust, could Decedent achieve the same tax result with a trust that qualifies for a marital deduction under Section 2056(b)(7)?

(c) Suppose Surviving Spouse strongly supports the same charity and intends to leave to that charity Surviving Spouse's entire estate. Can Decedent achieve the same tax result with a Section 2056(b)(5) life estate with a general power of appointment granted to Surviving Spouse or with an outright transfer?

(d) What are the advantages and disadvantages in using Section 2056(b)(8), Section 2056(b)(7), Section 2056(b)(5), or an outright transfer?

(10) Decedent's assets are as follows:

Property	*FMV at Death*	*FMV at Distribution*
Asset # 1	$3,500,000	$2,800,000
Asset # 2	3,500,000	2,000,000
Asset # 3	3,500,000	2,200,000
Asset # 4	3,500,000	7,000,000
	$14,000,000	$14,000,000

Decedent dies in the current year. Decedent's will gives Surviving Spouse the smallest pecuniary amount that will qualify for a marital deduction and will result in the smallest estate tax payable by Decedent's estate taking into consideration all deductions and credits. The provision further provides that such amount is to be satisfied by Personal Representative using cash, or any other assets Personal Representative chooses, valuing such assets at their date of death value. All other assets are transferred to a bypass trust. Assume Section 2056 is the only deduction provision.

(a) If the Personal Representative satisfies the bequest to Surviving Spouse with Assets #1, #2, and #3, will the bequest qualify for the marital deduction? See ¶ 5.06[6][a]; Rev. Proc. 64-19, 1964-1 (Part 1) CB 682.

(b) If, instead, the formula clause determines an amount that goes into the bypass trust to minimize taxes (with the excess passing to Surviving Spouse), the bypass trust amount is to be satisfied by the Personal Representative with cash or other property at its date of distribution value, and the Personal Representative transfers one half of Asset #4 to the bypass trust, will the property passing to Surviving Spouse qualify for the marital deduction? See Rev. Rul. 90-3, 1990-1 CB 175.

(11) Decedent has a potential taxable estate of $5 million. After establishing a bypass trust so as to utilize Decedent's applicable credit amount (see IRC § 2010), Decedent wants to leave Decedent's entire estate to Surviving Spouse, who is not a U.S. citizen.

(a) What must be done in order to qualify the remaining portion of Decedent's estate for a marital deduction? See IRC §§ 2056(d); 2056A.

(b) What tax consequences occur upon the death of the Surviving (noncitizen) Spouse?

PROBLEM 15

[SMLC&S refers to the abridged edition of Federal Estate and Gift Taxation (8th ed.). Appendix begins on page 103 of the Study Problems.]

Assignment

Code:	§§ 2010 (omit 2010(b)); 2011(a), 2011(f); 2012(a), 2012(e). Skim §§ 2001; 2013; 2014; 2015; 2016; 2058; 6018; 6075(a).
Regulations:	§§ 20.2013-1(a); 20.7520-3(b)(3)(i), 20.7520-3(b)(3)(ii).
SMLC&S:	¶¶ 1.02[5][c]–1.02[5][e]; 3.01; 3.02. Skim ¶¶ 2.01[1][a], 2.01[2], 2.01[3]; 2.02; 5.09.
Appendix:	Applicable Credit Amount Table.
Suggested References:	Rev. Rul. 59-9, 1959-1 CB 232.

Questions

(1) *D*, a U.S citizen who made no inter vivos gifts, died in the current year, leaving a gross estate of $3,000,000.

- **(a)** Will *D*'s executor be required to file a federal estate tax return?
- **(b)** Under what change of circumstances would a gross estate of this size require a return?
- **(c)** Since the tax liability of *D*'s estate is less than the Section 2010 credit, may the estate get a refund of excess credit?

(2) Consider the Section 2013 credit.

- **(a)** What is its purpose?
- **(b)** How do subsections (1) through (4) of Section 2013(a) complement that purpose?
- **(c)** How can there be a credit for estate tax paid with respect to a transfer of property to the decedent by a transferor who died as much

as two years after the death of the decedent, as expressly allowed by Section 2013(a)?

(3) Decedent *D* and Spouse *S*, neither having made any taxable gifts, each owns $4.5 million of assets. *D*, who predeceases *S* in the year 2009, leaves *D*'s property in trust with income to *S* for life, with a remainder to their child *C*. *S* dies within two years of *D* in the year 2010.

(a) Disregarding any application of Section 2013 (see question **(3)(b)**, below), consider the estate tax liability results to both estates (assuming no change in the value of the assets) (1) if *D*'s personal representative makes a QTIP election as to all of *D*'s property other than with respect to $3.5 million that passes to a bypass trust, or (2) if *D*'s personal representative does not make the election at *D*'s death.

(b) Assume that at *D*'s death, *S* is age 68, the applicable interest rate is 10 percent, and, as a result, *S*'s income interest is worth 70 percent of the corpus, and that *S* dies in 2010 within two years after *D*. Consider the estate tax liability results to both estates if *D*'s personal representative makes a QTIP election as to *D*'s property other than to $3.5 million that passes to a bypass trust, and, in the alternative, if the personal representative does not make a QTIP election. See IRC § 2013; Rev. Rul. 59-9 (cited in the assignment); Reg. § 20.7520-3(b)(3)(i).

PROBLEM 16

[SMLC&S refers to the abridged edition of Federal Estate and Gift Taxation (8th ed.).]

Assignment

Code:	§§ 2501(a)(1), 2501(a)(5); 2511(a). Skim §§ 1014; 1015; 7872(a), 7872(c)(1)(A), 7872(c)(2), 7872(d), 7872(e), 7872(f)(1)–7872(f)(7).
Regulations:	§§ 25.2511-1(a), 25.2511-1(e), 25.2511-1(f); 25.2511-2.
SMLC&S:	¶¶ 9.01; 9.02 (omit ¶ 9.02[1]); 10.01 (skim ¶ 10.01[3]; omit ¶¶ 10.01[10], 10.01[11]). Skim ¶ 8.10[3][a].
Suggested references:	Camp v. Comm'r, 195 F2d 999 (1st Cir. 1952), 52-1 USTC ¶ 10,849, 41 AFTR 1148. Dickman v. Comm'r, 465 US 330 (1984), 84-1 USTC ¶ 9240, 53 AFTR2d 1608. Galt v. Comm'r, 216 F2d 41 (7th Cir. 1954), 54-2 USTC ¶ 9457, 46 AFTR 633. Rev. Rul. 77-378, 1977-2 CB 347. Robinette v. Helvering, 318 US 184 (1943), 43-1 USTC ¶ 10,014, 30 AFTR 384.

Questions

(1) Following are some transactions that have been considered from the standpoint of their estate tax significance upon the death of the transferor. To what extent, if at all, do they constitute transfers subject to gift tax at the time of the transfer?

- **(a)** Near *D*'s death, which, as anticipated, occurred one year later, *D* gave an insurance policy on *D*'s life to Child *C*.
- **(b)** *D* transferred securities to a trust, retaining the right to the income for *D*'s life and providing for payment of the corpus at *D*'s death to unrelated *X* or *X*'s estate.

(c) *D* transferred securities to a trust under the terms of which the income was to be paid to unrelated *X* for *X*'s life. Upon *X*'s death, the corpus was to be returned to *D* if *D* was living, and, if not, it was to be paid over to unrelated *Y* or *Y*'s estate.

(d) *D* transferred securities to a trust under the terms of which the income was to be paid to *S* for *S*'s life. Upon *S*'s death, the remainder was to go to *X* or *X*'s estate. However, *D* retained an unlimited right to alter the terms of the trust in any manner.

(2) Remainderperson *R* owned a contingent remainder in a trust, which *R* transferred to *R*'s child. Under the trust terms, *R*'s sibling *S* was to receive the remainder if *S* survived the income beneficiary, and, if not, *R* or *R*'s estate was to receive the remainder. *R* paid a gift tax on the transfer, but one year later the income beneficiary died survived by *S*, and *R* sued for a refund of the gift tax. What is the result?

(3) Parent loans Child $1 million interest-free at a time when the Section 7872(f)(2) applicable federal rate is 10 percent. See IRC §§ 7872(a), 7872(c)(1), 7872(f)(2). Parent has a right to call the loan at any time Parent wishes and does so at the end of a year. Has Parent made any gift to Child?

(4) Prior to rendering services as personal representative of an estate, *PR* renounces any right to compensation. As a result, the $1,000 in fees *PR* would have earned passes to the residuary legatee of Decedent's estate.

(a) Has *PR* made a gift includable under Section 2511?

(b) Would *PR* make a gift if *PR* were the residuary taker of Decedent's estate? Why might *PR* renounce *PR*'s right to compensation?

(5) *D* creates a trust with income payable for *D*'s life either to *A* or to *B*, as *D* directs, remainder to *C* or *C*'s estate. *D* retains a power to revoke. Assume *A*, *B*, and *C* are unrelated to *D*.

(a) Does *D* make a completed gift at the time of creation of the trust?

(b) At *D*'s direction, the first year's income is paid equally to *A* and *B*. Are there any gifts?

(c) In addition, *D* relinquishes *D*'s power to revoke at the end of year 1, but not *D*'s right to direct income payments. Is there any further gift?

(d) In addition to the facts of question **(5)(c)**, above, at the end of year 2 *D* directs that year's income to be paid to *A* and effectively further directs that all remaining income during *D*'s life be paid to *A* or *A*'s estate. Are there any gifts?

(e) Would *D* have made a completed gift of the entire trust property if *D* had simply created a trust with income to *A* for ten years, remainder to *A* or *A*'s estate, and *D* retained a power to accumulate income?

(6) *D* creates a trust with income to *A* for *A*'s life, with a remainder to *B* or *B*'s estate. Discuss to what extent, if any, *D* has made a completed gift if *A*, *B*, and *C* are unrelated to *D* and:

(a) *D* retains a power to give income to *C*, but only with *A*'s approval.
(b) *D* retains no power over trust income, but does retain a power to make *C* or *C*'s estate the remainderperson if *D* secures *A*'s approval.
(c) *D* retains a power to give either the income or the remainder, or both, to *C*, but only with *A*'s approval.
(d) *D* retains a power to revoke the entire trust, but only with *A*'s approval.

(7) *D* creates a trust with an independent trustee, giving the trustee the power to give income to *A* or *B* for *D*'s life, with a remainder to *C* or *C*'s estate. *A*, *B*, and *C* are unrelated to *D*.

(a) To what extent has *D* made a completed gift?
(b) What is the result if, in addition, *D* provides that the independent trustee must give income necessary for *D*'s support and maintenance to *D* with any excess income in any year to go to *A* and *B*?
(c) What is the result in question **(7)(a)**, above, if, in addition, *D* provides that the independent trustee may, in the trustee's absolute discretion, distribute any or all of the corpus to *D*?

(8) In the current year, Donor holds two blocks of stock, both worth $100,000. Donor purchased the first block years ago for $10,000 and the second block more recently for $90,000. Donor plans to make an inter vivos gift of one block and retain the second until death. Which block of stock should Donor transfer and why?

PROBLEM 17

[SMLC&S refers to the abridged edition of Federal Estate and Gift Taxation (8th Ed.).]

Assignment

Code: §§ 2001(b); 2702 (omit § 2702(c)(4)); 6501(c)(9). Skim § 7520.

Regulations: §§ 25.2702-1; 25.2702-2 (omit §§ 25.2702-2(c), 25.2702-2(d) Exs. 8–10); 25.2702-3(a), 25.2702-3(b)(1)(i), 25.2702-3(b)(1)(iii), 25.2702-3(c)(1)(i), 25.2702-3(c)(1)(iii), 25.2702-3(d), 25.2702-3(f); 25.2702-4(a), 25.2702-4(c), 25.2702-4(d) Exs. 1–3; 25.2702-5(a), 25.2702-5(b)(1), 25.2702-5(c)(1), 25.2702-5(c)(2), 25.2702-5(d) Exs. 3, 4; 25.2702-6(a)(1), 25.2702-6(a)(2), 25.2702-6(b)(1).

SMLC&S: ¶ 19.03 (skim ¶¶ 19.03[2][c], 19.03[2][d]; omit ¶¶ 19.03[3][c], 19.03[4][b]–19.03[4][f]).

Questions

(1) Discuss the gift tax consequences of the following transfers:

(a) Grantor establishes an irrevocable trust with income to Grantor for ten years, and a remainder to Grantor's Child.

(b) Same as question **(1)(a)**, above, except that the remainder interest in the trust is given two thirds to Grantor's Child and one third to Grantor's Niece.

(c) Same as question **(1)(a)**, above, except that Grantor retains a power to alter the remainderperson from Child to Grandchildren. What are the consequences if, during the ten-year period, Grantor irrevocably names Child the remainderperson?

(d) Same as question **(1)(a)**, above, except that Child pays Grantor full and adequate consideration in money, or money's worth, for the remainder interest.

(e) Same as question **(1)(a)**, above, except that Grantor's Spouse is the income beneficiary of the trust for Spouse's life, with a remainder to their Child.

(f) Grantor establishes a trust with income to whomever of Grantor's Children Grantor selects each year, with a remainder to pass equally to Grantor's Grandchildren.

(g) What are the results in question **(1)(a)**, above, if two years after creating the trust, Grantor transfers Grantor's remaining interest in the trust to Child?

(2) Wealthy and Wealthy's Child purchase a piece of commercial property for $800,000; Wealthy pays $600,000 for a life estate in the property worth $600,000, and Child pays $200,000 for the remainder interest worth $200,000.

(a) Are there any gift tax consequences on the purchase?

(b) What are the gift tax consequences if Wealthy transfers to Child a remainder interest in the building that Wealthy owns for $200,000, the fair market value of the remainder?

(c) What are the estate tax consequences to Wealthy in **(2)(a)** and **(2)(b)**, above?

(3) Grantor establishes an irrevocable trust with income to Grantor for twelve years and a remainder to Grantor's Child.

(a) What are the results on creation of the trust if Grantor, in lieu of retaining the income for twelve years, retains that right to annual payments for twelve years equal to 6 percent of the original value of the trust corpus?

(b) What are the results on creation of the trust if Grantor, in lieu of retaining the income for twelve years, retains the right to annual payments for twelve years equal to 6 percent of the value of the trust corpus determined annually?

(c) What are the estate tax consequences in questions **(3)(a)** and **(3)(b)**, above, if Grantor dies within the twelve-year period?

(4) Grantor transfers an income interest in an irrevocable trust to Grantor's Parent for life with a reversion to Grantor.

(a) What are the gift tax consequences to Grantor?

(b) What is the result in question **(4)(a)**, above, if, each year, Parent is given 6 percent of the fair market value of the corpus of the trust at the time the trust was established?

(c) What is the result in question **(4)(b)**, above, if Grantor retains a reversion if Grantor survives Parent, but the property passes to unrelated *X* if Grantor does not?

(5) Wealthy and Wealthy's Child purchase a piece of commercial property for $800,000. Wealthy pays $600,000 for an annuity of $48,000 per year for Wealthy's life (6 percent of the $800,000 value of the property) worth $600,000, and Child pays $200,000 for the remainder interest worth $200,000. Are there any gift tax consequences on the purchase?

(6) Surviving Spouse, *S*, owns a family vacation home that *S* would like to continue to use for a few more years but would like to transfer to *S*'s two children at a minimal transfer tax cost.

(a) What are the results if *S* transfers the home to a qualified personal residence trust, retaining the right to the income for fifteen years (*S*'s life expectancy is twenty years) and a remainder to *S*'s children?

(b) What are the results if, in question **(6)(a)**, above, *S* also transfers the furnishings of the house to the trust?

(c) In general, would you advise *S* to use a regular personal residence trust or a qualified personal residence trust?

(d) What are the results if, in question **(6)(a)**, above, *S* dies after ten years?

(7) Wealthy and Wealthy's Child purchase a personal residence for $800,000; Wealthy pays $600,000 for a life estate worth $600,000, and Child pays $200,000 for the remainder interest worth $200,000.

(a) Are there any gift tax consequences on the purchase if the residence is a personal residence that is not held in a trust that Wealthy will use as a principal residence for life?

(b) What are the gift and estate tax results in question **(7)(a)**, above, if the residence is purchased and immediately put into a qualified personal residence trust with use of the residence to Wealthy for life and a remainder to Child?

(c) What are the gift and estate tax results to Wealthy if Wealthy transfers a previously owned personal residence worth $800,000 to a qualified personal residence trust, retaining use of the residence for life, and simultaneously sells the remainder interest in the trust, worth $200,000, to Child for $200,000?

PROBLEM 18

[*SMLC&S refers to the abridged edition of Federal Estate and Gift Taxation (8th ed.).*]

Assignment

Code: § 2512. Skim §§ 2503(e); 7517.

Regulations: §§ 25.2511-1(g)(1); 25.2512-1, 25.2512-8.

SMLC&S: ¶ 10.02 (skim ¶¶ 10.02[2][c], 10.02[2][d], 10.02[5]; omit ¶¶ 10.02[1][b], 10.02[2][b]).

Suggested references:

Comm'r v. Wemyss, 324 US 303 (1945), 45-1 USTC ¶ 10,179, 33 AFTR 584.

Diedrich v. Comm'r, 457 US 191 (1982), 82-1 USTC ¶ 9419, 50 AFTR2d 5054.

Estate of Sachs v. Comm'r, 88 TC 769 (1987), aff'd in part and rev'd in part, 856 F2d 1158 (8th Cir. 1988), 88-2 USTC ¶ 13,781, 62 AFTR2d 6000.

Rev. Rul. 93-12, 1993-1 CB 202.

Questions

(1) *A* and *B*, who are parent and child, respectively, own adjoining lots in a residential area, each worth $40,000. *A* needs $20,000 for personal use. *A* offers *B A*'s lot for $20,000, and *B* buys it for that price. Is there any gift?

(2) Should Section 2512(b) be viewed as a part of the definition of "gift" or as a measuring rod for transfers otherwise identified as gifts? For example, for several months *C* negotiated with a parent's sibling *T* for the purchase of 100 acres of *T*'s ranch. *T* finally sells the property to *C* for $1,900,000. If the Commissioner asserts, and it cannot be disproved, that the property was worth $2 million:

- **(a)** Has *T* made a gift? See Reg. § 25.2512-8.
- **(b)** Is *T*'s intent, donative or otherwise, entirely irrelevant?

(c) How does the test of a "gift," under the gift tax differ from the Section 102 test under the income tax?

(3) Donor transfers $50,000 of land with a $30,000 basis to Sibling on the condition that Sibling transfer $20,000 of cash to Parent. What are the gifts by Donor? By Sibling?

(4) In the current year, the following events occur. What are the gift tax consequences?

(a) Parent pays 22-year-old Child's law school expenses in the amount of $20,000.

(b) Parent gives 19-year-old Child $20,000 in cash, as agreed, if Child quits smoking, which child did.

(c) Parent gives 16-year-old Child a $60,000 automobile so that Child can get to and from high school.

(5) *D* owned an apartment building worth $1,500,000 that *D* wished to give to *B*. However, *D*'s cash position was poor, and *D* asked *B* if *B* would pay the gift tax if *D* gave *B* the building. This was agreed and done. Do not attempt a computation here, but, in general:

(a) How, if at all, should *B*'s payment of the gift tax affect the amount of *D*'s taxable gifts for the period?

(b) Would the result be different if there were no agreement that *B* would pay the tax, but the tax was collected from *B*? See IRC § 6324(b).

(c) What is the income tax result to *D* in question **(5)(a)**, above, if *D*'s adjusted basis in the building was $200,000 and *B* paid $500,000 of gift tax on the transfer?

(d) What is the estate tax result to *D* if *D* dies within three years of the transfer of the apartment building in question **(5)(a)**, above?

(6) Donor is the owner of limited partnership interests worth 60 percent of the value of the partnership as well as the general partnership interest worth another 20 percent of the value of the partnership. The partnership is worth $1 million. Donor gives each of Donor's three children one third of Donor's limited partnership interests. Discuss the value of the property transferred.

(7) **Community Property Question:** Spouses own $8 million of community property. At Decedent's death, Surviving Spouse elects under Decedent's will to take a life estate in all the community property, a remainder in all the property to their children. Due to Surviving Spouse's life expectancy, Surviving Spouse's life estate has a value of 50 percent at Decedent's death. At Surviving Spouse's death, the community property has appreciated to $10 million. See ¶ 4.08[7][c] for a discussion of the estate tax consequences.

(a) What are the estate tax consequences to Decedent, assuming Decedent's estate makes no Section 2056(b)(7) election?

(b) What are the gift and estate tax consequences to Surviving Spouse?

(c) How might any gift tax consequences to Surviving Spouse be avoided?

(d) What are the results in questions **(7)(a)** and **(7)(b)**, above, if Decedent's estate elects to use Section 2056(b)(7)? See United States v. Stapf, 375 US 118 (1963).

PROBLEM 19

[*SMLC&S refers to the abridged edition of Federal Estate and Gift Taxation (8th ed.).*]

Assignment

Code:	§ 2514 (omit §§ 2514(d), 2514(f)).
Regulations:	§§ 25.2514-1(a), 25.2514-1(b), 25.2514-3(a)–25.2514-3(c)(1), 25.2514-3(c)(3)–25.2514-3(c)(5).
SMLC&S:	¶ 10.04 (omit ¶¶ 10.04[3], 10.04[5]). Skim ¶ 4.13[5].
Suggested references:	Estate of Regester v. Comm'r, 83 TC 1 (1984).
	Self v. United States, 142 F. Supp. 939 (Ct. Cl. 1956), 56-2 USTC ¶ 11,613, 49 AFTR 1913.

Questions

(1) *D* is the life beneficiary of a trust. Under the terms of the trust instrument, there are no restrictions on *D*'s right to transfer *D*'s life interest to anyone *D* chooses.

- **(a)** The Service's position is that Section 2514 has no bearing on the tax consequences of *D*'s exercise of this right, even though it might aptly be termed a power of appointment. Why?
- **(b)** Is this to say that the exercise of *D*'s right is without gift tax consequences?

(2) Section 2514 treats the exercise of a general power of appointment as a "transfer of property." In determining the transfer tax consequences of the following problems, consider whether Congress should have more simply said that such an exercise constitutes a gift.

- **(a)** *D* exercises a general power by appointing one half of the corpus of a trust to *D*.
- **(b)** *D* exercises a general power by appointing the property subject to the power to a trust, the income to be paid to *D* for *D*'s life, with a remainder to *D*'s Child or Child's estate.

(c) *D*, the income beneficiary of a trust created by *X* with a remainder to *D*'s Sibling, has an unrestricted right to alter the terms of the trust. *D* names *D*'s Child rather than *D*'s Sibling as remainderperson of the trust, without relinquishing *D*'s right to make further alterations.

(d) Same as question **(2)(c)**, above, except that *D* relinquishes *D*'s right to make further alterations to the trust.

A parallel look at estate tax concepts is helpful here.

(3) In the current year, Decedent, by will, leaves Spouse a life interest in a trust with a power to appoint corpus to their children during Spouse's life, and a power to appoint to anyone by will. In the event Spouse fails to appoint the property, it will pass, at Spouse's death, to their children equally.

(a) Spouse exercises the power to appoint during Spouse's lifetime by appointing the entire corpus to Child. What are the gift tax consequences to Spouse?

(b) Spouse dies two years after the appointment in question **(3)(a)**, above. What are the estate tax consequences to Spouse's gross estate?

(c) What are estate tax consequences to Spouse's gross estate if Spouse dies and the power lapses?

(d) What are the estate tax consequences to Decedent's estate?

(4) Decedent was the income beneficiary of a trust created by Grantor with a remainder to *Z* or *Z*'s estate. *Z* is unrelated to Decedent. Decedent also had a noncumulative power to appoint to Decedent $15,000 per year out of the corpus of the trust, which at all times had a value of $200,000. The trust was created five years ago, and each year, by reason of nonexercise, the noncumulative power to appoint lapsed. These facts are similar to those of question **(5)(c)**, Problem 9.

(a) What are the gift tax consequences to Decedent in years 1 through 4 when Decedent's noncumulative power lapses?

(b) What is the difference in result if Decedent's Children, rather than *Z*, are the remainderpersons of the trust?

(c) What are the estate tax consequences to Decedent's estate in question **(4)(b)**, above, upon Decedent's death exactly five years after creation of the trust?

(d) What is the difference in result in question **(4)(c)**, above, if in year 5 the corpus of the trust appreciates from $200,000 to $300,000?

PROBLEM 20

[*SMLC&S refers to the abridged edition of Federal Estate and Gift Taxation (8th ed.).*]

Assignment

Code:	§§ 2043(b); 2516; 2518. Skim §§ 2034; 2053(c)(1)(A).
Regulations:	§§ 25.2516-1, 25.2516-2; 25.2518-2(a)–25.2518-2(c)(4)(i), 25.2518-2(c)(5) Exs. 1and 2, 25.2518-3(d) Exs. 2 and 21, 25.2518-2(e)(5) Exs. 4 and 5.
SMLC&S:	¶¶ 4.15[1]; 10.06; 10.07.
Suggested references:	McDonald v. Comm'r, 853 F2d 1494 (8th Cir. 1988), 88-2 USTC ¶ 13,778, 62 AFTR2d 5995.
	Merrill v. Fahs, 324 US 308 (1945), 45-1 USTC ¶ 10,180, 33 AFTR 587.
	Rev. Rul. 60-160, 1960-1 CB 374.
	Rev. Rul. 68-379, 1968-2 CB 414.

Questions

(1) Spouses *W* and *H* enter into a written separation agreement under which $550 per month is to be paid to *W* for *W*'s support during *W*'s life, plus $1,000 per month in child support until child *C*, now age 12, is 18. *W* also receives $30,000 in settlement of property rights in *H*'s estate, and, as a part of the agreement, *W* relinquishes all *W*'s marital rights, including *W*'s right to support. The future payments called for are a charge on *H*'s estate if *H* predeceases *W*.

- **(a)** What are the gift tax consequences if neither party seeks a divorce or separate maintenance decree?
- **(b)** What are the estate tax consequences if *H* died prior to any payment in question **(1)(a)**, above, with *W* and *C* surviving?
- **(c)** What are the gift tax consequences if a divorce is not final until three years after the agreement, but the agreement is conditional on court approval of the agreement, and it is approved with the court having power to accept or reject it?

(d) What are the estate tax consequences if *H* died prior to any payment in question **(1)(c)**, above, with *W* and *C* surviving?

(e) What are the gift tax consequences if the court has no power to approve or alter the agreement, but the divorce is final one year after the agreement?

(f) What are the estate tax consequences if *H* died prior to any payment in question **(1)(e)**, above, with *W* and *C* surviving?

(g) What are the gift tax consequences if a divorce is not final until three years after the agreement and the divorce court has no power to approve or alter the agreement?

(h) What are the estate tax consequences if *H* died after the divorce was final, but prior to any payment in question **(1)(g)**, above, with *W* and *C* surviving?

(2) In return for Spouse's marital rights (not support rights), *B*, pursuant to a written agreement entered into in the year of the divorce, subsequent to the divorce, creates a trust providing income to *B* for *B*'s life and a remainder to Spouse or Spouse's estate.

(a) On a transfer of property to the trust in the same year, does *B* make a gift?

(b) What are the consequences to *B*'s estate at *B*'s death, subsequent to the divorce?

(c) What are the gift tax consequences to *B* if a transfer is made to a trust that provides income to Spouse for fifteen years, reversion to *B* or *B*'s estate, and the transfer is pursuant to a written agreement entered into in the year of the divorce but it precedes the divorce? See IRC § 25.2702-1(c)(7).

(3) Donor created an irrevocable trust with income to be paid monthly for life to *A*, who is age 50, and provided *A* with a general testamentary power of appointment over the corpus of the trust. In default of appointment, the property passes to *B*, who is age 30, or *B*'s estate. Donor created the trust on January 1 of year 1, and *A* dies on January 1 of year 5. Assuming all the disclaimers in the following situations are in writing and are transmitted to the proper person, determine if each is a "qualified disclaimer" as described in Section 2518.

(a) *A* receives the first six months of income and, on August 1 of year 1, disclaims *A*'s income interest.

(b) *A* receives the first six months of income and, on August 1 of year 1, disclaims *A*'s general power of appointment.

(c) Same as question **(3)(b)**, above, except that *A* disclaims *A*'s general power to appoint over only one half of the property.

(d) On August 1 of year 1, *A* disclaims any right to exercise the general power in *A*'s or *A*'s estate's favor, thereby converting *A*'s general power of appointment to a nongeneral power.

(e) In view of *A*'s disclaimer on August 1 of year 1 in question **(3)(b)**, above, *B* disclaims *B*'s interest on December 1 of year 1.

(f) Same as question **(3)(e)**, above, except that *A* held a nongeneral power to appoint to anyone other than *A*, *A*'s estate, *A*'s creditors, or the creditors of *A*'s estate.

(g) Assume *A*, again, has a general power of appointment. *A* dies on January 1 of year 5, exercising *A*'s general power of appointment upon *A*'s death in favor of *C*. *C* disclaims on June 1 of year 5, prior to any receipt of the property.

(h) Same as question **(3)(g)**, above, except that *C* disclaims a remainder interest in the property but retains the right to income for *C*s life.

(4) Spouses, both U.S. citizens, owned real property in a joint tenancy funded by Decedent Spouse. At Decedent Spouse's death in the current year, Surviving Spouse would like to disclaim Surviving Spouse's survivorship interest in the property.

(a) Assuming the disclaimer occurs within nine months of Decedent Spouse's death, may Surviving Spouse successfully disclaim?

(b) What are the results if the property were held in a tenancy by the entirety?

(5) Decedent's will bequeaths Decedent's entire estate outright to Surviving Spouse. However, Decedent's will also provides that to the extent Surviving Spouse disclaims the property bequeathed outright, the property passes to a trust with income to Surviving Spouse for life with a remainder to whichever of their Children (or their estates) Surviving Spouse appoints and, on failure to appoint to the Children (or their estates), to the Children (or their estates) in equal shares. At the time Decedent's will was drafted, Decedent had assets worth approximately $800,000, but at death Decedent's gross estate is worth $4 million and Surviving Spouse has minimal assets. Surviving Spouse comes to you for advice. What do you advise?

PROBLEM 21

[*SMLC&S refers to the abridged edition of Federal Estate and Gift Taxation (8th ed.).*]

Assignment

Code:	§§ 529(c)(2), 529(c)(4), 529(c)(5); 2035(e), 2503; 6019(a); 6075(b).
Regulations:	§§ 25.2503-1, 25.2503-3, 25.2503-4, 25.2503-6.
SMLC&S:	¶ 9.04 (skim ¶¶ 9.04[7]–9.04[11]).
Suggested references:	Comm'r v. Herr, 303 F2d 780 (3d Cir. 1962), 62-2 USTC ¶ 12,079, 9 AFTR2d 1963.
	Crummey v. Comm'r, 397 F2d 82 (9th Cir. 1968), 68-2 USTC ¶ 12,541, 22 AFTR2d 6023.
	Estate of Cristofani v. Comm'r, 97 TC 74 (1991).
	Estate of Levine v. Comm'r, 526 F2d 717 (2d Cir. 1975), 76-1 USTC ¶ 13,115, 37 AFTR2d 1493.
	Hackl v. Comm'r, 118 TC 279 (2002), aff'd, 335 F3d 664 (7th Cir. 2003).
	Rev. Rul. 54-344, 1954-2 CB 319.
	Rev. Rul. 73-287, 1973-2 CB 321.
	Rev. Rul. 74-43, 1974-1 CB 285.

Questions

(1) Donor creates a trust with income to adult *A* for *A*'s life and a remainder to *B* or *B*'s estate. Does Donor make a gift of a "present interest" to either *A* or *B* if:

(a) Donor retains no powers?
(b) Donor makes *A*'s interest subject to a spendthrift clause?

(c) Donor names a third-party trustee, and the trustee holds a power to accumulate income?

(d) Donor names a third-party trustee, and the trustee holds a power under which trustee must give all income to *A* or *C* for *A*'s life, and a remainder to *B* or *B*'s estate?

(e) The third-party trustee in question **(1)(c)**, above, who holds a power to accumulate income can do so only with *A*'s approval?

(f) Donor in question **(1)(a)**, above, names a third-party trustee who holds a power to invade corpus only for *A*?

(2) *D*, a single taxpayer, transferred securities worth $20,000 to an irrevocable trust on August 1 of the current year, the first gift *D* ever made, providing for payment of the income to *A* for four years, and then a distribution of the remainder to *A* or *A*'s estate. Assume that at the time of the transfer, *A*'s income interest was properly valued at $5,000 and the remainder at $15,000.

(a) To what extent, if at all, can *D* claim an annual exclusion?

(b) What is the "total amount of gifts" made by *D* in the year?

(c) Might *D*'s gift tax be less if the income interest given to *A* was for a longer term of years?

(d) Is your answer to question **(2)(c)**, above, acceptable as a policy matter?

(e) If the transfer in question **(2)(a)**, above, was *D*'s only transfer for the year, would *D* be required to file a gift tax return for the year? If so, when would the return be due?

(3) *D*, a single taxpayer, is the owner of a policy of insurance on *D*'s own life, a "straight life" policy requiring annual $5,000 premium payments until *D*'s death.

(a) When the policy was properly valued at $75,000, *D* assigned all right, title, and interest in the policy irrevocably to child *C*. If this was *D*'s only gift-type transfer in the year, what was the "total amount of gifts" by *D* for the year?

(b) If, a year later, *D* paid the $5,000 premium on the policy previously assigned to *C*, would *D* have to file a gift tax return?

(c) What is the result in question **(3)(a)**, above, if *D* instead transferred the policy to a trust under which, when *D* died, the proceeds were to be invested and paid to *C* for life, with a remainder to *GC*, *C*'s child?

(d) What is the result in question **(3)(c)**, above, if *D* transferred $5,000 per year to the trust to pay the premiums on the policy?

(e) What is the result in question **(3)(d)**, above, if *D* also gave *C* the right, in each year, to take the $5,000 transfer from the trust and use it for any purpose *C* desires?

(f) What is the result in question **(3)(e)**, above, if the premium was $10,000, and *D* transferred $10,000 per year to the trust, giving *C* the right to demand the $10,000 per year? What are the estate tax consequences to *C*?

(g) What is the result in question **(3)(f)**, above, if *D* gives both *C* and *GC* the right to demand $5,000 each per year?

(h) What is the result in question **(3)(g)**, above, if the premium is $26,000 per year, *D* transferred $26,000 per year to the trust, giving both *C* and *GC* the right to demand $13,000 each per year? What are the estate tax consequences to *C* and *GC*?

(4) Parent *P* creates a trust for Child. Under the trust terms, the trustee is required to accumulate the income and distribute it to Child or Child's estate at the time Child reaches age 21. The corpus is to be paid to Child at age 21.

(a) Is there any exclusion in determining the total amount of gifts?

(b) What is the result in question **(4)(a)**, above, if the trustee was allowed either to accumulate the income or to expend the income or corpus for Child's benefit prior to Child's reaching age 21?

(c) Would your answer to question **(4)(b)**, above, be different if the trustee was authorized to expend trust income only for Child's college tuition?

(d) Would your answer to question **(4)(b)**, above, be different if the trust terms generally called for its continuance until Child attained age 25, but Child had the right to demand corpus and any accumulated income within the one-month period following Child's twenty-first birthday?

(e) Would your answer to any of the foregoing questions be different if required distributions were to take place when Child attained age 18 rather than age 21?

(f) Would your answer to question **(4)(b)**, above, be different if all accumulated income had to be paid out to Child when Child reached age 21, but no corpus distribution was required until Child attained age 25?

(g) In question **(4)(f)**, above, if the income interest prior to Child reaching age 21 was worth less than the Section 2503(b) annual exclusion, could Parent successfully argue that the value of the income interest during the period from when Child was age 21 to when Child reached age 25 also qualified for the annual exclusion?

(h) What is the result if the trustee has no power to accumulate income and it must be paid to Child until Child reaches age 25, when the corpus is to be distributed?

(5) Grandparent makes a $65,000 contribution to a Qualified Tuition Program for the benefit of Grandchild.

(a) Discuss the gift tax consequences to Grandparent. Does Section 2503(e) apply to the transfer? What is the result if Grandparent makes a Section 529(c)(2)(B) election?

(b) What are the gift tax results to Grandparent as distributions are made from the Qualified Tuition Program?

(c) What is the result to Grandparent in question **(5)(a)**, above, if Grandparent dies in the year after the year in which Grandparent made a Section 529(c)(2)(B) election?

(6) Individual, who is hurting both financially and physically, is given $15,000 by Friend in the current year to reimburse Individual for $8,000 of medical costs Individual incurred and to provide for Individual's support. What is the "total amount" of Friend's gift to Individual in the year? What should Friend have done here?

(7) Grantor creates a revocable living trust and subsequently makes several annual exclusion gifts from the trust. If Grantor dies within three years of making the annual exclusion gifts, are those gifts included with Grantor's gross estate?

PROBLEM 22

[SMLC&S refers to the abridged edition of Federal Estate and Gift Taxation (8th ed.).]

Assignment

Code:	§§ 2207A(b); 2519; 2522(a), 2522(c)(2); 2523; 2524; 6019(a). See §§ 2044; 2207A.
Regulations:	§§ 25.2519-1(a)–25.2519-1(g) Ex. 4; 25.2523(a)-1(a), 25.2523(a)-1(b), 25.2523(b)-1(a), 25.2523(b)-1(c), 25.2523(b)-1(d), 25.2523(f)-1(a)–25.2523(f)-1(c)(2).
SMLC&S:	¶¶ 11.01; 11.03 (skim ¶¶ 11.03[3], 11.03[4][a], 11.03[4][b]); 11.04. Skim ¶¶ 8.07; 10.08; 11.02.

Questions

(1) In the current year, Schemer gives $26,000 cash to charity and $26,000 cash to Child. Schemer claims to have made no taxable gifts, as shown below:

Gross gifts		$52,000
Exclusions (2)	$26,000	
Charitable deduction	26,000	
		52,000
Taxable gift		-0-

(a) What is Schemer overlooking?

(b) Will Schemer make a taxable gift if Schemer puts $26,000 cash in a trust with income to Child for a period of years (assume that Child's interest is worth $13,000), and a remainder to charity?

(2) Assuming Donor has made no other post-1976 transfers to Spouse, in which of the following circumstances, if any, would Donor be entitled to a gift tax marital deduction, and to what extent? Donor transfers property worth $20,000 to a trust. In each instance, assume the income interest is worth $13,000 at the time of the gift.

(a) The income to be paid to Parent for life, with a remainder to Spouse or Spouse's estate.

(b) The income to be paid to Spouse for life, with a remainder to Child or Child's estate. What additional facts do you need to know?

(c) The income to be paid to Spouse for ten years, with a remainder to Spouse or Spouse's estate.

(3) Determine the extent to which the gift tax marital deduction is available in the following transactions:

(a) Donor purchases, for $200,000, a parcel of real property for Donor and Spouse as joint tenants with right of survivorship.

(b) Donor places $100,000 in trust with income to Spouse for life, and a remainder to their children. In addition, Spouse is given a power to appoint the corpus to anyone by will.

(c) Is a gift tax return required to be filed in either question **(3)(a)** or question **(3)(b)**, above?

(4) Donor places $500,000 worth of closely held stock into an inter vivos trust with a qualifying income interest to Spouse for life and a remainder to the children of Donor's first marriage.

(a) What are the gift tax consequences to Donor if Donor makes a Section 2523(f) election?

(b) What are the gift tax consequences to Spouse in question **(4)(a)**, above, if Spouse gives the entire life estate to *X* prior to death?

(c) What are the estate tax consequences to Spouse in question **(4)(b)**, above?

(d) Is the result in question **(4)(b)**, above, fair to Spouse? To the children?

(e) What are the estate tax consequences to Spouse in question **(4)(a)**, above, if Spouse dies without making an inter vivos disposition of the life estate?

(f) What is the amount of gross estate inclusion in Spouse's gross estate if Spouse owns one third of the stock of closely held corporation outright and one third of the stock of closely held corporation is held in the trust in question **(4)(e)**, above. Assume each block of stock of closely held corporation is worth $500,000 before discounts and premiums and each would qualify for a combined minority and lack of marketability discounts (if applicable) of 40 percent.

(g) What are the gift tax consequences to Spouse in question **(4)(a)**, above, if Spouse gives one third of the life estate to unrelated *X* prior to death?

(h) What are the estate tax consequences to Spouse in question **(4)(f)**, above?

(5) Considering the fact that interspousal transfers can be made tax-free either during life or at death, is there any tax reason to make an inter vivos interspousal transfer as was done in question **(4)**, above?

PROBLEM 23

[*SMLC&S refers to the abridged edition of Federal Estate and Gift Taxation (8th ed.). Appendix begins on page 103 of the Study Problems.*]

Assignment

Code:	§§ 2001(c); 2502; 2505; 2513. Skim § 2504.
Regulations:	§§ 25.2504-1; 25.2513-1, 25.2513-4.
SMLC&S:	¶¶ 9.03; 9.06; 10.03. Skim ¶ 9.05.
Appendix:	Applicable Credit Amount Table.
Suggested reference:	Kass v. Comm'r, 16 TC 1035 (1957).

Questions

(1) Donor, who is married to Spouse, made the following gratuitous transfers in the current year. Donor transferred $40,000 to a trust, the income to be paid to Spouse for life, with a remainder to Child or Child's estate, but also gave the trustee the power within trustee's discretion to invade corpus for Spouse. Donor made no Section 2523(f) election. Donor also made a cash gift of $30,000 to Child. Using the annual exclusion and the split-gift provision, what would the "total amount of gifts" be for both Donor and Spouse as that term is used in Section 2503(a)?

(2) *A* has made numerous taxable gifts and by the current year has exhausted *A*'s Section 2505 credit. *A*'s spouse, *S*, has made none, and *S*'s credit is intact. In the current year, *A* gives child *C* $100,000. *A* and *S* then file a joint gift tax return for the calendar year in which the gift was made, escaping all tax by using *S*'s exclusion and credit. Is this the correct tax result?

(3) In the year 1997 when the applicable exclusion amount effectively was $600,000 and the Section 2505 credit was $192,800, after proper use of their annual exclusions, Donor made taxable gifts of $1 million, and Spouse made taxable gifts of $500,000. During the current year, Donor and Spouse make the following cash gifts and elect Section 2513:

Donor:	$806,000 to Child
	$ 61,000 to Spouse
	$102,000 to Charity
Spouse:	$246,000 to Sibling

Compute Donor's and Spouse's respective gift tax liabilities for the current year.

PROBLEM 24

[SMLC&S refers to the abridged edition of Federal Estate and Gift Taxation (8th ed.). Appendix begins on page 103 of the Study Problems.]

Assignment

Code:	§§ 2001; 2010; 2210(a); 2502; 2505. Skim §§ 2035; 2503(b).
SMLC&S:	Skim ¶¶ 2.01; 3.02; 8.10[1], 8.10[5]; 9.03; 9.05.
Appendix:	Applicable Credit Amount Table .

Questions

(1) Donor *D* died in the current year, owning property outright worth $4 million on the applicable valuation date (see IRC § 2504(b)). *D* had made no lifetime transfers accorded estate tax significance and had no other significant interests or powers. Assume there will be no estate tax deductions. Prior to the date of death, *D*, who was single, made the following outright cash gifts to *D*'s Cousin, the only gifts *D* ever made:

December 25, 2004	$1,011,000
December 25, 2005	$ 511,000

(a) Compute *D*'s gift tax liability in 2004 and 2005, and the federal estate tax liability for *D*'s estate. The annual exclusion was $11,000 in 2004 and 2005.

(2) Compute *D*'s estate tax liability if *D* previously made $1 million of taxable gifts after 1976 that were not included in *D*'s gross estate and *D* died in the current year with a $3.5 million taxable estate.

(3) Estate tax planning involves consideration of both the estate tax and the gift tax (as well as much more). The tax rates for those taxes are the same. Additionally, a credit to be applied against the two taxes is provided by Sections 2010 and 2505. The two taxes are closely related, but the integration is not complete. In the circumstances below, compute and compare the total transfer taxes a donor or decedent would pay (assuming that no deductions, exclusions, etc., including Section 2503(b), are available) and the net amount the donees or beneficiaries would receive if the Donor or Decedent had assets worth $8 million, if the Donor or Decedent made no prior gifts, and if:

(a) *D* held the assets until death in the current year.

(b) *D* gave away one half of the assets, paid the gift tax out of the remaining assets, and held the remaining assets until death more than three years later.

(c) Same as question **(3)(b)**, above, except that death occurred within three years of the date of gift.

PROBLEM 25

[*SMLC&S refers to the abridged edition of Federal Estate and Gift Taxation (8th ed.).*]

Assignment

Code:	§§ 2701 (skim §§ 2701(d), 2701(e)(3), 2701(e)(7)); 2704; 6501(c)(9).
Regulations:	§§ 25.2701 (omit §§ 25.2701-1(b)(2)(ii); 25.2701-3(b)–25.2701-3(d); 25.2701-4; 25.2701-5; 25.2701-6; 25.2701-7); 25.2704. Skim Reg. §§ 25.2701-5(a)(1), 25.2701-5(b).
SMLC&S:	¶¶ 19.02 (skim ¶¶ 19.02[2][d], 19.02[4][a]–19.02[4][c], 19.02[4][f], 19.02[5][a]; omit ¶¶ 19.02[4][d], 19.02[4][e], 19.02[5][b]–19.02[5][g]); 19.05 (omit ¶ 19.05[4]).
Suggested Reference:	Harrison v. Comm'r, 52 TCM (CCH) 1306 (1987).

Questions

(1) Transferor *T* owns all of *X* corporation's common stock worth $1 million. In a nontaxable corporate reorganization, *T* transfers *T*'s common stock in exchange for 1,000 shares of nonvoting preferred stock with a noncumulative 10 percent dividend per year, and 1,000 shares of common stock. The preferred stock has a $1,000 par value but can be sold to the corporation for $800 per share at any time. The preferred stock has a fair market value of $1 million. *T* transfers *T*'s 1,000 shares of common stock to *T*'s child *C* immediately after the reorganization. Ten years later, at *T*'s death, *X* corporation is worth $1.8 million, *T*'s preferred stock is valued at $1 million, and *C*s common stock is valued at $800,000.

- **(a)** Disregarding Section 2701, what are the gift tax consequences to *T* upon the transfer of the common stock to *C*, and what are the estate tax consequences to *T* at *T*'s death?
- **(b)** What are the gift tax consequences to *T* under Section 2701? What are the estate tax consequences to *T*?

(c) What are the gift tax consequences in question **(1)(b)**, above, if the common stock is worth $100,000, the preferred stock is worth $900,000, and *C* purchases the common stock from *T* for $100,000?

(d) What are the gift tax consequences in question **(1)(b)**, above, if both the common and the preferred stock have a readily available market value on an established securities market on the date of the transfer?

(e) What are the gift tax consequences in question **(1)(b)**, above, if *T* transfers only 50 percent of each class of stock to *C*?

(f) What are the gift tax consequences in question **(1)(b)**, above, if *T* transfers only 50 percent of the preferred stock (and no common stock) to *C*?

(g) What are the gift tax consequences in question **(1)(b)**, above, if *T* transfers the preferred stock to *T*'s Spouse at the time of the gift of the common stock to *C*?

(h) What are the gift tax consequences in question **(1)(b)**, above, if *T* owns only 10 percent of the corporation?

(2) Assume the same facts as in question **(1)**, above, except that *T*'s right to the preferred stock dividends is a cumulative right worth $950,000, and *T* has a right at any time to sell the preferred stock to the corporation for $800,000.

(a) What are the gift tax consequences to *T* upon the transfer of the common stock to *C*?

(b) What are the results in question **(2)(a)**, above, if the sale price is $925,000 (rather than $800,000)?

(c) What are the results in question **(2)(a)**, above, if *T* elects to waive qualified payment treatment of the cumulative dividend right? See IRC § 2701(c)(3)(C)(i). Why might *T* make the election?

(3) Taxpayer owns real estate worth $1 million that Taxpayer transfers to a corporation in a corporate formation in return for preferred stock worth $1 million. The preferred stock has a noncumulative 10 percent dividend and a right to sell the stock to the corporation for $1 million. Taxpayer's child transfers $100,000 of cash to the corporation in return for all of the common stock of the corporation, which is worth $100,000. What are the gift tax consequences to Taxpayer as a result of the corporate formation?

(4) Parent and Child each own general and limited partnership interests in the Parent-Child partnership. Each general partner has the right to require the partnership to liquidate, except that Parent's right expires at Parent's death. What are the Section 2704 consequences at Parent's death?

(5) Parent and Child are equal partners in the Parent-Child partnership. The partnership agreement provides that the partnership cannot be terminated.

- **(a)** Parent dies and bequeaths Parent's partnership interest to Child. What is the value of Parent's partnership interest in Parent's gross estate?
- **(b)** What are the results in question **(5)(a)**, above, if Unrelated Lender required the agreement not to terminate during the term of a loan that Lender made to the partnership? Such a requirement is common practice in the community.

PROBLEM 26

[*SMLC&S refers to the abridged edition of Federal Estate and Gift Taxation (8th ed.).*]

Assignment

Code:	§§ 2613; 2651; 2652(a)(1), 2652(b), 2652(c). Skim §§ 2601; 2611(a); 2612.
Regulations:	§§ 26.2612-1(d); 26.2652-1(b).
SMLC&S:	¶¶ 1.04; 12.01; 13.03; 17.01; 17.02[1][a], 17.02[1][b], 17.02[3][a], 17.02[3][b].

Questions

(1) Which of the following entities may be skip persons?

- **(a)** A trust.
- **(b)** A corporation.
- **(c)** An estate.

(2) Which of the following persons are skip persons? Assume in each question that the parents of Grandchild are living unless stated otherwise.

- **(a)** Transferor's Child.
- **(b)** Transferor's Grandchild.
- **(c)** Transferor's Spouse.
- **(d)** Transferor's Grandchild whose parent was a lineal descendant of the Transferor and is deceased.
- **(e)** Transferor's Spouse's Child by a prior marriage.
- **(f)** Transferor's Adopted Child's Child. What is the result if Transferor also adopts Adopted Child's Child?
- **(g)** Transferor's Grandchild's Spouse.
- **(h)** Transferor's Significant Other, who is age 30 (Transferor is age 45).
- **(i)** Same as question **(2)(h)**, above, except Transferor is age 70 and quite lively.
- **(j)** Fifty-year-old Transferor's Significant Other's Child. What do you need to know?
- **(k)** Transferor, age 70, adopts Significant Other's ten-year-old Child.

(3) A trust created by Grantor provides for income to *A* for *A*'s life, with a remainder to *B* or *B*'s estate. *T*, the trustee, holds a power to give income to *C* for *C*'s support and maintenance if *T* deems it necessary.

(a) Does *T*, *A*, *B*, or *C* hold a Section 2652(c) interest in the trust?
(b) If *D* is given a power to invade corpus for *D*, does *D* hold a Section 2652(c) interest in the trust?

(4) Transferor makes an irrevocable transfer to a trust. Assume in each question that the parents of Grandchild are living. Does the trust constitute a skip person if:

(a) The income from the trust is to be paid to Transferor's Child for life, with a remainder to Transferor's Grandchildren?
(b) The income from the trust is to be paid to Transferor's Grandchild for life, with a remainder to Transferor's Great-Grandchildren?
(c) The income from the trust is to be paid to Transferor's Grandchild until age 40, with a remainder to Transferor's Grandchild if living and, if Grandchild is not living, to Grandchild's Aunt?
(d) The income from the trust is to be paid to Transferor's Grandchild until age 40, with a remainder to Grandchild or Grandchild's estate; however, prior to Grandchild reaching age 40, an independent trustee may invade corpus for Transferor's Child?
(e) The income from the trust is to be accumulated for ten years and then distributed to Transferor's Grandchild or Grandchild's estate?
(f) The income from the trust is to be accumulated for ten years and then distributed to Transferor's Child or Transferor's Grandchildren, whomever the independent trustee selects?

PROBLEM 27

[*SMLC&S refers to the abridged edition of Federal Estate and Gift Taxation (8th ed.).*]

Assignment

Code:	§§ 2611; 2612; 2651(e); 2653(a); 2654(b)(2). Skim §§ 2613; 2651; 2652(a)(l).
Regulations:	§§ 26.2612-1(a); 26.2612-1(b)(1)(i); 26.2612-1(f) Exs. 2, 6, 13; 26.2653-1(b) Ex. 1.
SMLC&S:	¶¶ 13.01; 13.02 (skim ¶¶ 13.02[2][f], 13.02[2][g], 13.02[3][c]; omit ¶¶ 13.02[2][e], 13.02[4][c], 13.02[4][d]); 17.03[1]. Skim ¶ 17.04[2].

Questions

(1) Which of the following constitute direct skips? Assume in each question that the parents of Grandchild are living unless stated otherwise.

- **(a)** Donor makes an inter vivos transfer of property to Donor's Child.
- **(b)** Donor makes an inter vivos transfer of property to Donor's Grandchild.
- **(c)** Donor makes an inter vivos transfer of property to Donor's Great-Grandchild.
- **(d)** Decedent bequeaths property to Decedent's Grandchild.
- **(e)** Donor makes an inter vivos transfer of property to Donor's Grandchild, but Grandchild's Parent (Donor's Child) is dead and Grandchild is being raised by Grandchild's Other Parent.
- **(f)** Donor makes a transfer of property to a trust with income to Grandchild for ten years, and a remainder to Grandchild or Grandchild's estate.
- **(g)** Same as question **(1)(f)**, above, except the trust is revocable.
- **(h)** Same as question **(1)(f)**, above, but Grandchild's Parent (Donor's Child) is dead.
- **(i)** Donor pays Grandchild's law school tuition.

(2) Grantor establishes a testamentary trust with income to Spouse for life, then income to Child for life, then income to Grandchildren for life, with a remainder to Great-Grandchildren.

(a) Does the creation of the trust result in a direct skip?

(b) Is there a taxable termination at Spouse's death if Child survives?

(c) Is there a taxable termination at Spouse's death if Child predeceases Spouse?

(d) Is there a taxable termination at Child's death if Child survives Spouse?

(e) Would your answer in question **(2)(d)**, above, be different if Child had a general power to appoint the trust property, but Child failed to appoint and, on the default of appointment, the trust continued as originally provided?

(f) Same as question **(2)(d)**, above, except that the trustee has a power to sprinkle corpus to Grandchildren after Child's death and does so. Is there a taxable distribution? See IRC §§ 2612(b), 2653(a).

(g) Assuming that Grantor has two grandchildren, and Spouse and Child predecease Grandchildren, is there a taxable termination on the death of the grandchild who dies first? See IRC § 2654(b)(2). Is there a taxable termination on the death of the surviving grandchild?

(3) Grantor establishes an inter vivos trust providing for income to Grantor for life, and a remainder to Grantor's Grandchild.

(a) What are the Chapter 13 consequences upon creation of the trust?

(b) What are the Chapter 13 consequences when Grantor dies survived by Grandchild's Parent who is Grantor's Child?

(c) What are the Chapter 13 consequences when Grantor dies if Grandchild's Parent dies before the trust is established?

(4) Grantor of the trust in question **(2)**, above, wishes to avoid the generation-skipping transfer tax.

(a) Would Grantor be successful if Grantor gave the trustee a sprinkling power over the corpus for Grandchildren during Child's life, and the trustee exercised the power by giving 50 percent of the corpus to Grandchildren?

(b) What are the Chapter 13 consequences if the trustee invaded the entire corpus for Grandchildren?

(c) What if the trustee had a power to invade corpus to pay Grandchildren's college tuition, and the trustee exercised that power?

(5) Grantor establishes a trust with income to Grandchild for five years, to be used primarily for Grandchild's education expenses, then income to Grandchild's Parent (Grantors' Child) for life, and a remainder to Grandchild.

- **(a)** What are the Chapter 13 consequences to the trust?
- **(b)** What are the Chapter 13 consequences if Grantor makes an outright $100,000 inter vivos gift to Grandchild whose parents are alive, and, several years later, when Grantor's Spouse is financially in trouble, Grandchild gives the $100,000 to Grantor's Spouse who lives off the income of the $100,000 during Spouse's life and then bequeaths it to Grandchild?

(6) Is there a generation-skipping transfer in the following situations:

- **(a)** Grantor creates a trust with income to Child for life, and a remainder to whichever of Grantor's Grandchildren Child selects by will, with the remainder passing to the Grandchildren equally if Child fails to select any Grandchildren. Child makes no selection by will.
- **(b)** Same as question **(6)(a)**, above, except that Child may also appoint the property by will to the creditor of Child's estate.
- **(c)** The trust is the same as question **(6)(a)**, above, except that Grantor also gives one Grandchild a power to appoint the corpus to anyone during Child's life. Grandchild appoints the property outright to Child.

PROBLEM 28

[SMLC&S refers to the abridged edition of Federal Estate and Gift Taxation (8th ed.). Appendix begins on page 103 of the Study Problems.]

Assignment

Code:	§§ 2515; 2601; 2602; 2603; 2621; 2622; 2623; 2624; 2631; 2632; 2641; 2642(a), 2642(c); 2652(a)(2); 2653(b)(1); 2662. Skim § 2513.
Regulations:	§ 26.2662-1(c).
SMLC&S:	¶¶ 10.05; 12.02; 12.03[1]; 14.01; 15.01; 15.02; 16.01; 17.02[1][c][ii]. Skim ¶¶ 14.02[1]; 14.03[1]; 14.04[1]; 14.05[1]; 15.03[1], 15.03[3][a], 15.03[4][a], 15.03[4][b], 15.03[5]; 16.02[2][a]–16.02[2][b][iii], 16.02[2][c], 16.02[3]; 17.03[2][a]; 18.02[1]–18.02[4].
Appendix:	Applicable Credit Amount Table.

Questions

(1) Assume for ease of computation that there is a flat estate and gift tax rate of 45 percent, there is no annual exclusion or zero inclusion amount, and there is no appreciation in the value of the property between the time of the original transfer and any subsequent tax imposition. Determine the total taxes payable if Donor, without using any exemptions or credits, makes the following transfers:

- **(a)** Donor makes an inter vivos $2 million gift to Donor's Grandchild, and Donor pays all taxes. See IRC § 2515.
- **(b)** Donor transfers $4 million to an inter vivos trust with income to Child for life and a remainder to Grandchild.

(2) Each year, Donor makes an inter vivos $13,000 outright gift to each of Donor's nineteen grandchildren. In addition, Donor pays one of Donor's grandchildren's $18,000 law school tuition.

- **(a)** What is Donor's total gift tax and generation-skipping transfer tax liability?

(b) Most of Donor's nineteen grandchildren are very young and Donor would prefer to give them $13,000 per year in trust without incurring any gift or generation-skipping transfer tax. What must Donor do to achieve this result?

(3) In the current year, Donor makes a $600,000 outright transfer to Donor's Grandchild, whose parents are living. Donor has previously used up Donor's Section 2631 generation-skipping transfer exemption.

(a) What is Donor's Chapter 13 tax liability?

(b) What is the result in question **(3)(a)**, above, if the transfer is to a trust that provides income to Grandchild for life, with a remainder to Grandchild's Children?

(4) Grandparent has made no previous gratuitous transfers. How much of Grandparent's GST exemption will be automatically allocated to the following transfers which occurred in the current year:

(a) Grandparent made a $500,000 inter vivos direct skip to Grandchild.

(b) Grandparent transferred $500,000 to an inter vivos trust providing income to Child for life and remainder to Grandchild or Grandchild's estate.

(c) Grandparent died at the end of the current year. Grandparent's will bequeaths $50,000 outright to Grandchild and provides that the residue of Grandparent's estate passes to a trust providing income to Child for life and a remainder to Grandchild or Grandchild's estate.

(5) In 2004, Transferor, who had made no previous gratuitous transfers, created a trust that provided income to Transferor's Child until age 45 with a remainder to Child at age 45, but with a contingent remainder to Grandchildren if Child dies prior to age 45. Transferor made no allocation of GST exemption to the trust and none was deemed allocated. In current year, Child predeceased Transferor, resulting in a taxable termination. At the time of creation of the trust, the value of the property transferred was $3.5 million and at the time of Child's death, it was $7 million.

(a) What can Transferor do to minimize the generation-skipping transfer tax liability?

(b) Would the result in question **(5)(a)**, above, be altered if the trust was established in 1996 rather than 2004?

(6) Decedent, who is unmarried and has never made any inter vivos transfers, dies in 2009 and leaves Decedent's entire estate, $3.5 million, in trust with income to Child for life, then income to Grandchildren for life, and a remainder to Great-Grandchildren with an appropriate perpetuities savings clause.

(a) Child dies when the trust corpus is valued at $6 million. What is the amount of the generation-skipping transfer tax liability?

(b) Decedent, although wanting to save wealth transfer taxes, is primarily concerned with Child's welfare. What additional powers or interests may Decedent give Child without jeopardizing wealth transfer tax consequences?

(c) Grandchildren who survive child die when the corpus is worth $20 million. What is the amount of generation-skipping transfer tax liability?

(7) During life, Decedent transferred property to Grandchild and used $1 million of Decedent's Section 2631 exemption. At Decedent's death in 2009, after payment of estate taxes, Decedent transfers the $7.5 million residue of Decedent's estate in trust with income to Child for life, then income to Grandchild for life, and a remainder to Grandchild's children. Assume a 50 percent maximum federal estate tax rate.

(a) How much generation-skipping transfer tax is due at Child's death in 2010 if the corpus is then worth $10 million?

(b) How much generation-skipping transfer tax is due at Grandchild's death in 2015, assuming Grandchild survives Child, if the corpus is then worth $15 million?

(8) Grandparent, having previously made no other gratuitous transfers, gives Grandchild $4 million in current year, and Grandparent elects to use Section 2513. What is the Chapter 13 tax liability on the transfer?

(9) Consider the following procedural aspects of the generation-skipping transfer tax:

(a) Who is liable for the generation-skipping transfer tax, and what resources are generally used to pay the tax?

(b) Who must file a generation-skipping transfer tax return and when?

PROBLEM 29

[SMLC&S refers to the abridged edition of Federal Estate and Gift Taxation (8th ed.). Appendix begins on page 103 of the Study Problems.]

Assignment

Code:	§§ 2652(a)(1), 2652(a)(3). Skim §§ 2001(b); 2010(c); 2044; 2056(b)(7); 2631; 2651(e).
Regulations:	§§ 20.2056(b)–20.2056(b)(2)(ii); 26.2612-1(f) Ex. 4; 26.2652-1(a)(5) Ex. 6, 26.2652-2; 26.2654-1(a)(1)(ii); 26.2654-1(b)(1).
SMLC&S:	¶ 17.02[1][c][i].
Appendix:	Applicable Credit Amount Table.

Questions

(1) **(a)** If Decedent leaves property in trust and Decedent's executor makes a Section 2056(b)(7) QTIP election, who is the transferor of any interest in the QTIP after either Section 2519 or Section 2044 applies?

(b) What does Section 2652(a)(3) do?

(c) Who makes the Section 2652(a)(3) election?

(d) If Decedent in question **(1)(a)**, above, provides for the remainder interest in the trust to pass to Grandchild, what type of generation-skipping transfer occurs at Surviving Spouse's death if a Section 2652(a)(3) election is not made? What is the result if a Section 2652(a)(3) election is made?

(e) May a Section 2652(a)(3) election be made to only a portion of a trust?

(f) What is the principal reason for use of a Section 2652(a)(3) election?

(2) Decedent has a $4 million estate remaining after making an inter vivos taxable gift of $1 million in 2002 to Child. Decedent's Spouse has a minimal estate. Decedent creates a single revocable inter vivos trust that, at Decedent's death, is to be split into three identical trusts with income to Spouse for life, then income to Child for life, with a remainder to Child's Children. The first trust is to be funded with assets equal to the applicable exclusion amount reduced by the amount of the applicable exclusion amount used during the Decedent's lifetime under Section 2505. The second trust is to be funded with assets equal to the Decedent's unused GST exemption amount less the amount funded in the first trust. The residue goes into the third trust. Any expenses or claims are to be paid out of the residue prior to funding the third trust. The successor trustee of Decedent's trust is to make a QTIP election with respect to the second and third trusts, to make a Section 2653(a)(3) election as to the second trust, and to allocate Decedent's unused Section 2631 GST exemption to the first and second trusts.

(a) What estate-planning goal is Decedent attempting to accomplish?

(b) If Decedent had created only a single trust, may the successor trustee split the trust into the three trusts above, make a QTIP election with respect to the second and third trusts, and make a Section 2652(a)(3) reverse QTIP election with respect to the second trust?

PROBLEM 30

[SMLC&S refers to the abridged edition of Federal Estate and Gift Taxation (8th ed.).]

Assignment

Code:	§§ 2642(f)(1), 2642(f)(3); 2654(a), 2654(c); 2661. See Tax Reform Act of 1986, §§ 1433(b)–1433(d), as amended. Generally, these Act sections may be found in the fine print following Section 2601 in the Code. Skim §§ 1014(a)(1), 1014(b)(9); 1015(d)(1), 1015(d)(6); 2515.
Regulations:	§§ 26.2601-1(a), 26.2601-1(b)(1)(ii)(A)–26.2601-1(b)(1)(ii)(C); 26.2601-1(b)(1)(i), 26.2601-1(b)(1)(iv)(A), 26.2601-1(b)(1)(iv)(B), 26.2601-1(b)(1)(v)(B); 26.2601-1(b)(2)(i); 26.2632-1(c)(1).
SMLC&S:	¶¶ 16.02[7][a], 16.02[7][d]; 17.04[1], 17.04[3]. Skim ¶¶ 18.01[1]; 18.05.

Questions

(1) Grantor purchased a parcel of land for $100,000 and had the title conveyed to Grantor and Grandchild as joint tenants with right of survivorship. Grandchild's parents are both living. Grantor's residuary estate passes to Grandchild's Children. Grantor predeceases Grandchild.

- **(a)** What are the gift and estate tax consequences to Grantor if the land is worth $200,000 at Grantor's death?
- **(b)** What are the Chapter 13 consequences to Grantor and when do they occur?
- **(c)** What is Grandchild's income tax basis in the land after Grantor's death?
- **(d)** If Grandchild (who has already used up the Section 2505 credit) has married a wealthy person and has no need for the land, may Grandchild disclaim Grandchild's one-half survivorship interest in the land at Grantor's death and have the land pass to Grandchild's Children under the residuary clause of Grantor's will? See question **(4)** of Problem 20.

(2) Grantor makes an inter vivos direct skip transfer of property with an adjusted basis of $100,000 and a fair market value of $500,000 to Grandchild, whose parents are both alive. Disregarding any Section 2503(b) consequences and assuming a flat 50 percent Chapter 12 tax rate and Chapter 13 applicable rate, determine Grandchild's adjusted basis in the property for income tax purposes. See IRC §§ 1015(d)(1), 1015(d)(6); 2515.

(3) What is the function of Section 2661?

(4) Grantor creates an irrevocable inter vivos trust with income to Child and a remainder to Grandchild.

- **(a)** If the trust was created and funded on January 1, 1985, is its corpus subject to the generation-skipping transfer tax?
- **(b)** What is the result in question **(4)(a)**, above, if the income Beneficiary of the trust has a nongeneral power of appointment over the trust remainder that Beneficiary exercises, providing income to Beneficiary's Child (who was alive at the time of the creation of the trust) for life, and a remainder to Beneficiary's Grandchild?
- **(c)** If the trust was created and funded on January 1, 1986, is its corpus subject to the generation-skipping transfer tax?
- **(d)** If an additional transfer is made on January 1, 1988, to the corpus of the trust described in question **(4)(a)**, above, is the trust subject to the generation-skipping transfer tax?
- **(e)** If the trust was created by a will drafted on January 1, 1986, and Decedent died in 1986 without amending the will, is the trust subject to the tax imposed by Chapter 13?

APPENDIX

APPLICABLE CREDIT AMOUNT TABLE SECTION 2010

Year of Death	*Applicable Exclusion Amount*	*Applicable Credit Amount*
1987–1997	$ 600,000	$ 192,800
1998	$ 625,000	$ 202,050
1999	$ 650,000	$ 211,300
2000–2001	$ 675.000	$ 220,550
2002–2003	$1,000,000	$ 345,800
2004–2005	$1,500,000	$ 555,800
2006–2008	$2,000,000	$ 780,800
2009	$3,500,000	$1,455,800
2010	—	—
2011 or thereafter	$1,000,000	$ 345,800

APPLICABLE CREDIT AMOUNT TABLE SECTION 2505

Year of Death	*Applicable Exclusion Amount*	*Applicable Credit Amount*
1987–1997	$ 600,000	$ 192,800
1998	$ 625,000	$ 202,050
1999	$ 650,000	$ 211,300
2000–2001	$ 675,000	$ 220,550
2002 or therafter	$1,000,000	$ 345,800

VALUATION TABLES

Table S

Based on Life Table 2000CM
Single Life Remainder Factors
Applicable on or After May 1, 2009
Interest Rate

Age	0.2%	0.4%	0.6%	0.8%	1.0%	1.2%	1.4%	1.6%	1.8%	2.0%
0	.85816	.73751	.63478	.54723	.47252	.40872	.35416	.30747	.26745	.23313
1	.85889	.73863	.63604	.54844	.47355	.40948	.35459	.30752	.26711	.23239
2	.86054	.74145	.63968	.55260	.47802	.41409	.35922	.31209	.27155	.23664
3	.86221	.74433	.64339	.55687	.48263	.41887	.36404	.31685	.27619	.24112
4	.86390	.74725	.64716	.56121	.48733	.42374	.36898	.32175	.28098	.24575
5	.86560	.75018	.65097	.56561	.49209	.42871	.37401	.32675	.28588	.25050
6	.86731	.75314	.65482	.57006	.49692	.43375	.37913	.33186	.29090	.25538
7	.86902	.75611	.65868	.57454	.50180	.43885	.38432	.33704	.29601	.26035
8	.87073	.75909	.66258	.57907	.50674	.44403	.38960	.34233	.30122	.26544
9	.87246	.76209	.66651	.58364	.51173	.44928	.39497	.34771	.30654	.27064
10	.87419	.76511	.67046	.58826	.51679	.45459	.40042	.35319	.31197	.27596
11	.87592	.76814	.67445	.59291	.52190	.45998	.40596	.35876	.31750	.28139
12	.87766	.77119	.67845	.59761	.52706	.46544	.41157	.36443	.32313	.28693
13	.87939	.77424	.68247	.60232	.53225	.47094	.41723	.37015	.32884	.29255
14	.88112	.77728	.68649	.60704	.53746	.47646	.42293	.37592	.33460	.29823
15	.88284	.78031	.69050	.61176	.54267	.48199	.42865	.38172	.34038	.30394
16	.88455	.78333	.69449	.61647	.54788	.48752	.43437	.38752	.34619	.30968
17	.88625	.78633	.69848	.62117	.55309	.49307	.44012	.39336	.35203	.31546
18	.88795	.78933	.70246	.62588	.55830	.49863	.44589	.39923	.35791	.32129
19	.88964	.79232	.70644	.63059	.56354	.50422	.45170	.40514	.36385	.32719
20	.89132	.79532	.71044	.63534	.56882	.50987	.45757	.41114	.36987	.33317
21	.89301	.79832	.71445	.64010	.57413	.51555	.46350	.41719	.37597	.33925
22	.89470	.80133	.71847	.64488	.57947	.52129	.46948	.42332	.38216	.34541
23	.89639	.80434	.72251	.64970	.58486	.52708	.47554	.42954	.38844	.35168
24	.89808	.80737	.72658	.65456	.59031	.53295	.48169	.43586	.39484	.35809
25	.89978	.81042	.73068	.65947	.59583	.53890	.48795	.44230	.40137	.36464
26	.90149	.81349	.73482	.66443	.60141	.54494	.49430	.44886	.40804	.37134
27	.90320	.81657	.73899	.66944	.60707	.55107	.50076	.45554	.41484	.37819
28	.90492	.81968	.74319	.67450	.61278	.55728	.50733	.46233	.42178	.38520
29	.90665	.82279	.74741	.67960	.61856	.56356	.51398	.46924	.42884	.39233
30	.90837	.82591	.75165	.68473	.62438	.56990	.52070	.47623	.43601	.39959

Age	0.2%	0.4%	0.6%	0.8%	1.0%	1.2%	1.4%	1.6%	1.8%	2.0%
31 ..	.91010	.82904	.75592	.68989	.63024	.57631	.52751	.48333	.44329	.40698
32 ..	.91182	.83218	.76020	.69509	.63616	.58278	.53440	.49052	.45068	.41449
33 ..	.91355	.83532	.76449	.70031	.64212	.58931	.54137	.49780	.45818	.42213
34 ..	.91527	.83847	.76880	.70556	.64811	.59589	.54839	.50516	.46578	.42988
35 ..	.91700	.84162	.77312	.71082	.65414	.60253	.55549	.51261	.47347	.43774
36 ..	.91872	.84477	.77744	.71611	.66021	.60921	.56266	.52014	.48127	.44572
37 ..	.92043	.84792	.78178	.72142	.66631	.61594	.56989	.52774	.48916	.45381
38 ..	.92215	.85107	.78613	.72675	.67244	.62272	.57718	.53544	.49715	.46201
39 ..	.92386	.85422	.79048	.73210	.67860	.62955	.58453	.54320	.50523	.47032
40 ..	.92557	.85736	.79483	.73746	.68479	.63641	.59194	.55104	.51340	.47873
41 ..	.92727	.86050	.79918	.74283	.69100	.64331	.59940	.55894	.52165	.48724
42 ..	.92896	.86364	.80354	.74820	.69723	.65024	.60690	.56691	.52998	.49585
43 ..	.93065	.86677	.80789	.75359	.70348	.65721	.61447	.57495	.53840	.50457
44 ..	.93234	.86990	.81225	.75899	.70976	.66422	.62208	.58305	.54690	.51338
45 ..	.93402	.87302	.81660	.76439	.71605	.67125	.62973	.59122	.55547	.52228
46 ..	.93569	.87613	.82095	.76980	.72236	.67832	.63743	.59945	.56413	.53129
47 ..	.93735	.87924	.82530	.77521	.72867	.68541	.64517	.60773	.57286	.54037
48 ..	.93901	.88233	.82964	.78062	.73501	.69253	.65295	.61606	.58166	.54955
49 ..	.94065	.88541	.83397	.78604	.74135	.69967	.66077	.62446	.59053	.55882
50 ..	.94229	.88849	.83830	.79145	.74771	.70684	.66864	.63292	.59949	.56819
51 ..	.94393	.89156	.84263	.79688	.75409	.71404	.67655	.64143	.60852	.57766
52 ..	.94556	.89462	.84695	.80230	.76048	.72127	.68450	.65001	.61763	.58722
53 ..	.94717	.89767	.85126	.80772	.76687	.72852	.69249	.65863	.62680	.59687
54 ..	.94878	.90070	.85555	.81313	.77326	.73577	.70050	.66730	.63603	.60658
55 ..	.95037	.90371	.85983	.81853	.77964	.74302	.70851	.67598	.64530	.61635
56 ..	.95195	.90670	.86406	.82388	.78599	.75024	.71651	.68465	.65457	.62613
57 ..	.95351	.90965	.86827	.82920	.79230	.75744	.72448	.69332	.66384	.63593
58 ..	.95505	.91257	.87243	.83447	.79857	.76459	.73242	.70195	.67309	.64573
59 ..	.95657	.91546	.87655	.83970	.80479	.77170	.74033	.71057	.68233	.65553
60 ..	.95807	.91832	.88064	.84490	.81098	.77879	.74822	.71918	.69158	.66534
61 ..	.95955	.92115	.88469	.85005	.81713	.78584	.75608	.72776	.70081	.67515
62 ..	.96101	.92395	.88869	.85515	.82323	.79283	.76388	.73630	.71001	.68494
63 ..	.96245	.92670	.89265	.86020	.82926	.79977	.77164	.74479	.71917	.69470
64 ..	.96387	.92942	.89655	.86518	.83524	.80665	.77933	.75323	.72828	.70443
65 ..	.96527	.93210	.90040	.87011	.84116	.81346	.78697	.76162	.73735	.71411
66 ..	.96665	.93476	.90423	.87502	.84706	.82027	.79461	.77002	.74645	.72385
67 ..	.96802	.93739	.90803	.87990	.85292	.82705	.80223	.77841	.75554	.73359
68 ..	.96937	.93999	.91179	.88472	.85874	.83378	.80980	.78676	.76461	.74331
69 ..	.97070	.94255	.91549	.88949	.86449	.84044	.81731	.79504	.77362	.75299
70 ..	.97200	.94506	.91914	.89419	.87016	.84702	.82473	.80326	.78256	.76260

Age	0.2%	0.4%	0.6%	0.8%	1.0%	1.2%	1.4%	1.6%	1.8%	2.0%
71 ..	.97328	.94754	.92273	.89882	.87577	.85353	.83209	.81140	.79143	.77215
72 ..	.97453	.94997	.92626	.90338	.88129	.85996	.83935	.81945	.80021	.78162
73 ..	.97576	.95234	.92972	.90785	.88671	.86627	.84651	.82739	.80888	.79098
74 ..	.97695	.95466	.93310	.91223	.89202	.87247	.85353	.83518	.81741	.80019
75 ..	.97811	.95692	.93638	.91649	.89720	.87851	.86039	.84281	.82577	.80923
76 ..	.97924	.95910	.93957	.92063	.90224	.88440	.86708	.85026	.83393	.81807
77 ..	.98033	.96122	.94267	.92465	.90715	.89013	.87360	.85753	.84191	.82671
78 ..	.98138	.96327	.94567	.92855	.91190	.89571	.87995	.86461	.84968	.83515
79 ..	.98239	.96526	.94857	.93233	.91652	.90112	.88611	.87149	.85725	.84337
80 ..	.98337	.96717	.95138	.93598	.92098	.90635	.89208	.87817	.86460	.85135
81 ..	.98431	.96901	.95408	.93951	.92529	.91141	.89786	.88463	.87172	.85910
82 ..	.98521	.97077	.95667	.94290	.92944	.91629	.90344	.89088	.87861	.86660
83 ..	.98608	.97247	.95917	.94616	.93343	.92099	.90882	.89691	.88526	.87385
84 ..	.98691	.97409	.96156	.94928	.93727	.92551	.91399	.90271	.89166	.88084
85 ..	.98770	.97565	.96384	.95228	.94094	.92984	.91895	.90828	.89782	.88757
86 ..	.98845	.97713	.96602	.95514	.94446	.93398	.92371	.91362	.90373	.89402
87 ..	.98917	.97854	.96810	.95786	.94781	.93794	.92825	.91873	.90939	.90021
88 ..	.98985	.97988	.97008	.96046	.95100	.94171	.93258	.92361	.91479	.90612
89 ..	.99049	.98115	.97196	.96292	.95404	.94530	.93671	.92826	.91994	.91176
90 ..	.99110	.98235	.97373	.96526	.95691	.94871	.94062	.93267	.92484	.91713
91 ..	.99168	.98348	.97541	.96747	.95964	.95193	.94434	.93686	.92949	.92223
92 ..	.99222	.98455	.97700	.96955	.96222	.95498	.94785	.94083	.93390	.92707
93 ..	.99273	.98556	.97849	.97152	.96464	.95786	.95117	.94457	.93806	.93163
94 ..	.99321	.98651	.97989	.97337	.96692	.96057	.95429	.94810	.94199	.93595
95 ..	.99366	.98739	.98121	.97510	.96907	.96312	.95724	.95143	.94569	.94002
96 ..	.99408	.98822	.98244	.97673	.97108	.96551	.95999	.95454	.94916	.94384
97 ..	.99447	.98900	.98359	.97825	.97297	.96774	.96258	.95747	.95242	.94742
98 ..	.99483	.98973	.98467	.97967	.97473	.96984	.96500	.96021	.95547	.95078
99 ..	.99518	.99040	.98568	.98101	.97638	.97180	.96727	.96278	.95834	.95394
100	.99549	.99103	.98661	.98224	.97791	.97362	.96937	.96516	.96100	.95687
101	.99579	.99162	.98750	.98340	.97935	.97534	.97136	.96742	.96351	.95964
102	.99607	.99217	.98831	.98448	.98068	.97692	.97319	.96950	.96583	.96220
103	.99634	.99271	.98911	.98553	.98199	.97848	.97500	.97155	.96812	.96473
104	.99659	.99320	.98984	.98651	.98320	.97992	.97666	.97344	.97023	.96705
105	.99683	.99369	.99056	.98747	.98439	.98134	.97830	.97530	.97231	.96934
106	.99713	.99429	.99146	.98865	.98586	.98309	.98033	.97760	.97488	.97218
107	.99747	.99496	.99246	.98998	.98751	.98506	.98262	.98020	.97779	.97539
108	.99800	.99602	.99404	.99208	.99012	.98818	.98624	.98431	.98240	.98049
109	.99900	.99801	.99702	.99603	.99505	.99407	.99310	.99213	.99116	.99020

Age	2.2%	2.4%	2.6%	2.8%	3.0%	3.2%	3.4%	3.6%	3.8%	4.0%
0 ...	.20365	.17830	.15648	.13767	.12144	.10741	.09528	.08476	.07564	.06772
1 ...	.20251	.17677	.15458	.13542	.11885	.10451	.09209	.08131	.07194	.06379
2 ...	.20656	.18060	.15817	.13877	.12197	.10740	.09476	.08376	.07420	.06586
3 ...	.21084	.18466	.16200	.14236	.12533	.11054	.09767	.08647	.07670	.06817
4 ...	.21527	.18888	.16600	.14613	.12887	.11385	.10076	.08935	.07938	.07066
5 ...	.21984	.19324	.17013	.15004	.13255	.11730	.10399	.09237	.08220	.07329
6 ...	.22454	.19773	.17440	.15408	.13636	.12089	.10736	.09553	.08515	.07605
7 ...	.22933	.20233	.17879	.15824	.14030	.12460	.11085	.09880	.08822	.07892
8 ...	.23425	.20705	.18330	.16254	.14436	.12844	.11447	.10221	.09142	.08193
9 ...	.23930	.21191	.18795	.16697	.14857	.13243	.11824	.10576	.09476	.08507
10 ..	.24446	.21689	.19273	.17153	.15292	.13655	.12214	.10945	.09824	.08835
11 ..	.24975	.22200	.19764	.17623	.15740	.14081	.12619	.11328	.10187	.09177
12 ..	.25515	.22724	.20268	.18107	.16202	.14521	.13037	.11724	.10563	.09533
13 ..	.26064	.23256	.20782	.18600	.16674	.14972	.13466	.12132	.10949	.09900
14 ..	.26620	.23796	.21303	.19101	.17154	.15430	.13903	.12547	.11344	.10273
15 ..	.27179	.24340	.21829	.19607	.17639	.15894	.14344	.12968	.11743	.10652
16 ..	.27742	.24887	.22358	.20117	.18128	.16361	.14790	.13391	.12145	.11034
17 ..	.28309	.25439	.22893	.20632	.18622	.16834	.15241	.13821	.12554	.11421
18 ..	.28881	.25997	.23434	.21154	.19123	.17314	.15699	.14258	.12969	.11815
19 ..	.29461	.26563	.23983	.21684	.19633	.17803	.16167	.14703	.13393	.12218
20 ..	.30050	.27139	.24543	.22226	.20156	.18304	.16646	.15161	.13829	.12633
21 ..	.30649	.27726	.25114	.22779	.20689	.18817	.17138	.15631	.14277	.13060
22 ..	.31259	.28323	.25697	.23344	.21235	.19342	.17642	.16114	.14739	.13500
23 ..	.31879	.28934	.26293	.23923	.21795	.19882	.18161	.16612	.15215	.13955
24 ..	.32515	.29559	.26904	.24519	.22372	.20440	.18699	.17128	.15710	.14429
25 ..	.33166	.30201	.27534	.25133	.22969	.21018	.19256	.17665	.16226	.14924
26 ..	.33833	.30861	.28182	.25767	.23586	.21616	.19835	.18224	.16764	.15440
27 ..	.34517	.31538	.28849	.26420	.24224	.22236	.20436	.18804	.17324	.15980
28 ..	.35217	.32233	.29535	.27093	.24882	.22877	.21058	.19407	.17907	.16542
29 ..	.35932	.32944	.30237	.27784	.25558	.23537	.21701	.20031	.18511	.17126
30 ..	.36661	.33670	.30956	.28492	.26253	.24216	.22362	.20674	.19135	.17730
31 ..	.37403	.34411	.31691	.29217	.26965	.24914	.23044	.21338	.19779	.18355
32 ..	.38160	.35167	.32442	.29960	.27697	.25631	.23745	.22022	.20445	.19002
33 ..	.38930	.35939	.33211	.30721	.28447	.26368	.24467	.22727	.21133	.19671
34 ..	.39713	.36724	.33993	.31497	.29213	.27123	.25207	.23451	.21839	.20360
35 ..	.40509	.37523	.34792	.32290	.29998	.27896	.25967	.24195	.22567	.21070
36 ..	.41318	.38337	.35606	.33100	.30800	.28688	.26746	.24961	.23317	.21803
37 ..	.42139	.39165	.36435	.33927	.31621	.29499	.27546	.25746	.24087	.22557
38 ..	.42974	.40008	.37281	.34771	.32460	.30330	.28366	.26554	.24880	.23334
39 ..	.43821	.40864	.38141	.35631	.33316	.31179	.29205	.27381	.25694	.24133

Age	2.2%	2.4%	2.6%	2.8%	3.0%	3.2%	3.4%	3.6%	3.8%	4.0%
40 ..	.44679	.41734	.39016	.36507	.34189	.32046	.30064	.28229	.26529	.24954
41 ..	.45549	.42616	.39906	.37399	.35080	.32932	.30942	.29097	.27386	.25797
42 ..	.46430	.43511	.40809	.38307	.35987	.33836	.31840	.29986	.28264	.26662
43 ..	.47324	.44421	.41729	.39232	.36913	.34760	.32758	.30897	.29165	.27552
44 ..	.48229	.45343	.42663	.40172	.37857	.35702	.33697	.31829	.30088	.28465
45 ..	.49144	.46277	.43611	.41128	.38817	.36663	.34655	.32782	.31033	.29400
46 ..	.50072	.47225	.44574	.42101	.39796	.37644	.35634	.33757	.32002	.30360
47 ..	.51009	.48185	.45550	.43089	.40791	.38642	.36633	.34753	.32992	.31343
48 ..	.51958	.49158	.46540	.44093	.41803	.39660	.37652	.35770	.34006	.32351
49 ..	.52917	.50143	.47545	.45113	.42833	.40696	.38691	.36810	.35043	.33383
50 ..	.53888	.51141	.48566	.46150	.43883	.41754	.39754	.37874	.36106	.34442
51 ..	.54871	.52153	.49602	.47204	.44951	.42832	.40838	.38961	.37194	.35528
52 ..	.55865	.53179	.50653	.48276	.46038	.43931	.41945	.40073	.38307	.36641
53 ..	.56869	.54217	.51718	.49363	.47143	.45050	.43074	.41208	.39446	.37781
54 ..	.57882	.55265	.52796	.50465	.48265	.46186	.44222	.42364	.40607	.38945
55 ..	.58902	.56322	.53884	.51579	.49400	.47338	.45387	.43540	.41789	.40131
56 ..	.59926	.57383	.54978	.52701	.50544	.48501	.46565	.44729	.42987	.41335
57 ..	.60951	.58449	.56078	.53830	.51698	.49675	.47755	.45932	.44201	.42555
58 ..	.61978	.59517	.57182	.54964	.52858	.50858	.48956	.47147	.45427	.43790
59 ..	.63007	.60589	.58290	.56105	.54027	.52050	.50167	.48375	.46668	.45041
60 ..	.64039	.61665	.59405	.57254	.55205	.53253	.51392	.49617	.47925	.46310
61 ..	.65072	.62743	.60524	.58409	.56390	.54465	.52627	.50872	.49196	.47595
62 ..	.66104	.63822	.61645	.59566	.57581	.55683	.53870	.52136	.50478	.48892
63 ..	.67133	.64900	.62766	.60726	.58774	.56907	.55120	.53409	.51770	.50200
64 ..	.68161	.65977	.63887	.61887	.59970	.58134	.56375	.54688	.53071	.51519
65 ..	.69186	.67053	.65009	.63049	.61170	.59367	.57637	.55976	.54381	.52849
66 ..	.70216	.68136	.66140	.64223	.62383	.60615	.58916	.57283	.55713	.54203
67 ..	.71250	.69224	.67277	.65405	.63605	.61874	.60208	.58605	.57062	.55575
68 ..	.72283	.70312	.68416	.66590	.64833	.63140	.61509	.59938	.58423	.56963
69 ..	.73312	.71398	.69553	.67776	.66062	.64409	.62815	.61277	.59793	.58360
70 ..	.74335	.72479	.70688	.68959	.67291	.65680	.64124	.62621	.61168	.59764
71 ..	.75353	.73556	.71819	.70141	.68519	.66951	.65434	.63968	.62549	.61176
72 ..	.76364	.74626	.72945	.71318	.69744	.68220	.66745	.65317	.63933	.62593
73 ..	.77365	.75686	.74061	.72487	.70962	.69484	.68051	.66662	.65315	.64009
74 ..	.78350	.76733	.75164	.73643	.72167	.70735	.69346	.67997	.66688	.65417
75 ..	.79318	.77761	.76249	.74781	.73355	.71971	.70625	.69318	.68048	.66813
76 ..	.80266	.78769	.77314	.75899	.74524	.73187	.71886	.70621	.69390	.68192
77 ..	.81194	.79756	.78358	.76997	.75672	.74382	.73127	.71904	.70713	.69553
78 ..	.82100	.80722	.79380	.78072	.76798	.75556	.74346	.73166	.72016	.70894
79 ..	.82984	.81664	.80378	.79124	.77900	.76706	.75542	.74405	.73296	.72213

Age	2.2%	2.4%	2.6%	2.8%	3.0%	3.2%	3.4%	3.6%	3.8%	4.0%
80 ..	.83843	.82582	.81351	.80149	.78976	.77830	.76711	.75618	.74550	.73507
81 ..	.84678	.83474	.82298	.81148	.80025	.78927	.77853	.76803	.75777	.74773
82 ..	.85487	.84339	.83217	.82119	.81045	.79994	.78966	.77959	.76974	.76009
83 ..	.86269	.85177	.84107	.83060	.82035	.81030	.80047	.79083	.78139	.77214
84 ..	.87024	.85986	.84968	.83970	.82993	.82035	.81095	.80174	.79271	.78385
85 ..	.87751	.86765	.85798	.84849	.83919	.83005	.82110	.81230	.80368	.79521
86 ..	.88450	.87515	.86597	.85696	.84811	.83942	.83089	.82251	.81428	.80619
87 ..	.89119	.88234	.87363	.86508	.85668	.84843	.84031	.83234	.82450	.81679
88 ..	.89760	.88922	.88099	.87289	.86492	.85708	.84938	.84180	.83434	.82700
89 ..	.90372	.89580	.88801	.88034	.87280	.86537	.85806	.85087	.84378	.83681
90 ..	.90954	.90207	.89471	.88746	.88032	.87329	.86637	.85954	.85282	.84620
91 ..	.91508	.90803	.90109	.89424	.88750	.88085	.87429	.86783	.86146	.85518
92 ..	.92033	.91369	.90714	.90068	.89432	.88803	.88184	.87572	.86969	.86374
93 ..	.92530	.91904	.91287	.90678	.90078	.89484	.88899	.88321	.87751	.87188
94 ..	.92999	.92411	.91830	.91256	.90690	.90130	.89578	.89032	.88493	.87961
95 ..	.93442	.92889	.92342	.91802	.91269	.90741	.90220	.89706	.89197	.88694
96 ..	.93858	.93338	.92824	.92316	.91813	.91316	.90825	.90340	.89859	.89385
97 ..	.94248	.93759	.93276	.92798	.92325	.91857	.91395	.90937	.90484	.90036
98 ..	.94614	.94155	.93701	.93252	.92807	.92367	.91931	.91500	.91073	.90650
99 ..	.94959	.94528	.94101	.93679	.93260	.92846	.92436	.92030	.91628	.91229
100	.95278	.94874	.94473	.94075	.93682	.93292	.92906	.92523	.92144	.91769
101	.95581	.95201	.94824	.94451	.94081	.93715	.93352	.92992	.92635	.92281
102	.95860	.95503	.95149	.94798	.94450	.94105	.93763	.93424	.93088	.92754
103	.96136	.95802	.95470	.95142	.94816	.94492	.94171	.93853	.93538	.93224
104	.96390	.96077	.95766	.95458	.95152	.94848	.94547	.94248	.93951	.93657
105	.96640	.96347	.96057	.95769	.95483	.95199	.94917	.94637	.94359	.94083
106	.96950	.96684	.96420	.96157	.95896	.95636	.95379	.95123	.94868	.94616
107	.97301	.97064	.96829	.96595	.96362	.96131	.95901	.95672	.95445	.95219
108	.97859	.97670	.97482	.97295	.97109	.96923	.96739	.96555	.96373	.96191
109	.98924	.98828	.98733	.98638	.98544	.98450	.98356	.98263	.98170	.98077

Age	4.2%	4.4%	4.6%	4.8%	5.0%	5.2%	5.4%	5.6%	5.8%	6.0%
0 ...	.06083	.05483	.04959	.04501	.04101	.03749	.03441	.03170	.02931	.02721
1 ...	.05668	.05049	.04507	.04034	.03618	.03254	.02934	.02652	.02403	.02183
2 ...	.05858	.05222	.04665	.04178	.03750	.03373	.03042	.02750	.02492	.02264
3 ...	.06072	.05420	.04848	.04346	.03904	.03516	.03173	.02871	.02603	.02366
4 ...	.06303	.05634	.05046	.04530	.04075	.03674	.03319	.03006	.02729	.02483
5 ...	.06547	.05861	.05258	.04726	.04258	.03844	.03478	.03153	.02866	.02610

Age	4.2%	4.4%	4.6%	4.8%	5.0%	5.2%	5.4%	5.6%	5.8%	6.0%
6 ...	.06805	.06102	.05482	.04935	.04453	.04026	.03647	.03312	.03014	.02749
7 ...	.07074	.06353	.05717	.05155	.04658	.04217	.03826	.03479	.03171	.02895
8 ...	.07356	.06617	.05964	.05386	.04875	.04421	.04017	.03658	.03338	.03053
9 ...	.07651	.06895	.06225	.05631	.05105	.04637	.04220	.03849	.03518	.03222
10 ..	.07960	.07185	.06499	.05889	.05347	.04865	.04435	.04052	.03709	.03402
11 ..	.08283	.07490	.06786	.06160	.05603	.05106	.04663	.04267	.03912	.03594
12 ..	.08620	.07808	.07087	.06444	.05871	.05360	.04903	.04494	.04127	.03798
13 ..	.08967	.08137	.07397	.06738	.06149	.05623	.05152	.04729	.04351	.04010
14 ..	.09321	.08472	.07715	.07038	.06433	.05892	.05406	.04971	.04579	.04227
15 ..	.09680	.08812	.08036	.07342	.06721	.06164	.05664	.05214	.04810	.04445
16 ..	.10041	.09154	.08360	.07649	.07011	.06438	.05923	.05459	.05041	.04664
17 ..	.10409	.09502	.08689	.07960	.07305	.06716	.06185	.05707	.05276	.04886
18 ..	.10782	.09855	.09024	.08276	.07604	.06998	.06452	.05959	.05514	.05111
19 ..	.11164	.10217	.09366	.08600	.07910	.07288	.06726	.06218	.05758	.05341
20 ..	.11559	.10592	.09721	.08937	.08228	.07589	.07010	.06487	.06012	.05582
21 ..	.11965	.10977	.10087	.09283	.08557	.07900	.07305	.06765	.06276	.05831
22 ..	.12383	.11376	.10465	.09642	.08897	.08223	.07610	.07055	.06550	.06090
23 ..	.12817	.11789	.10859	.10016	.09252	.08559	.07930	.07358	.06837	.06363
24 ..	.13270	.12221	.11270	.10408	.09625	.08914	.08267	.07678	.07141	.06651
25 ..	.13744	.12674	.11703	.10821	.10019	.09289	.08625	.08018	.07465	.06960
26 ..	.14239	.13149	.12158	.11256	.10435	.09686	.09003	.08380	.07810	.07288
27 ..	.14758	.13647	.12636	.11714	.10873	.10106	.09405	.08764	.08177	.07639
28 ..	.15300	.14169	.13137	.12195	.11335	.10549	.09829	.09171	.08567	.08012
29 ..	.15864	.14712	.13660	.12698	.11819	.11013	.10275	.09598	.08977	.08406
30 ..	.16448	.15275	.14203	.13222	.12323	.11498	.10742	.10047	.09408	.08820
31 ..	.17053	.15861	.14769	.13768	.12849	.12006	.11230	.10517	.09860	.09255
32 ..	.17680	.16468	.15357	.14336	.13398	.12535	.11741	.11009	.10335	.09712
33 ..	.18330	.17099	.15968	.14927	.13970	.13088	.12275	.11525	.10832	.10192
34 ..	.19000	.17750	.16599	.15539	.14562	.13661	.12829	.12061	.11350	.10693
35 ..	.19692	.18423	.17253	.16174	.15178	.14258	.13408	.12621	.11892	.11217
36 ..	.20407	.19119	.17931	.16833	.15818	.14879	.14009	.13204	.12457	.11764
37 ..	.21144	.19838	.18631	.17515	.16481	.15523	.14635	.13811	.13046	.12335
38 ..	.21904	.20582	.19357	.18222	.17170	.16193	.15287	.14444	.13661	.12932
39 ..	.22687	.21348	.20105	.18952	.17882	.16887	.15962	.15102	.14300	.13554
40 ..	.23493	.22137	.20878	.19707	.18619	.17606	.16663	.15784	.14965	.14201
41 ..	.24322	.22950	.21674	.20487	.19381	.18350	.17390	.16493	.15656	.14873
42 ..	.25173	.23786	.22494	.21290	.20168	.19120	.18141	.17227	.16372	.15572
43 ..	.26049	.24648	.23342	.22122	.20982	.19918	.18922	.17990	.17118	.16301
44 ..	.26950	.25535	.24214	.22979	.21824	.20742	.19730	.18781	.17892	.17057
45 ..	.27874	.26447	.25112	.23862	.22692	.21595	.20566	.19600	.18694	.17843

Age	4.2%	4.4%	4.6%	4.8%	5.0%	5.2%	5.4%	5.6%	5.8%	6.0%
46 ..	.28824	.27385	.26038	.24774	.23589	.22476	.21431	.20450	.19527	.18659
47 ..	.29798	.28349	.26989	.25712	.24513	.23386	.22326	.21328	.20390	.19505
48 ..	.30797	.29338	.27967	.26678	.25466	.24325	.23250	.22238	.21283	.20383
49 ..	.31822	.30355	.28974	.27674	.26449	.25294	.24206	.23179	.22210	.21294
50 ..	.32876	.31401	.30011	.28701	.27465	.26298	.25196	.24156	.23172	.22242
51 ..	.33958	.32477	.31079	.29759	.28513	.27335	.26221	.25168	.24170	.23226
52 ..	.35068	.33582	.32178	.30851	.29595	.28407	.27282	.26216	.25206	.24249
53 ..	.36206	.34717	.33308	.31974	.30710	.29513	.28378	.27301	.26279	.25309
54 ..	.37371	.35880	.34467	.33127	.31857	.30651	.29507	.28420	.27388	.26406
55 ..	.38559	.37067	.35652	.34308	.33032	.31820	.30668	.29572	.28529	.27537
56 ..	.39765	.38275	.36859	.35512	.34232	.33014	.31855	.30751	.29699	.28697
57 ..	.40990	.39502	.38086	.36739	.35455	.34233	.33068	.31957	.30898	.29887
58 ..	.42231	.40747	.39333	.37985	.36700	.35474	.34304	.33188	.32121	.31103
59 ..	.43490	.42011	.40600	.39253	.37968	.36740	.35567	.34446	.33374	.32348
60 ..	.44768	.43296	.41890	.40546	.39261	.38033	.36858	.35733	.34656	.33625
61 ..	.46064	.44600	.43200	.41860	.40578	.39351	.38175	.37048	.35968	.34933
62 ..	.47373	.45920	.44527	.43194	.41915	.40690	.39514	.38387	.37305	.36267
63 ..	.48696	.47253	.45870	.44544	.43271	.42049	.40876	.39749	.38666	.37625
64 ..	.50030	.48601	.47229	.45911	.44645	.43428	.42258	.41133	.40051	.39010
65 ..	.51377	.49963	.48603	.47295	.46037	.44827	.43662	.42540	.41460	.40420
66 ..	.52750	.51352	.50007	.48711	.47464	.46262	.45103	.43987	.42911	.41872
67 ..	.54144	.52765	.51436	.50154	.48919	.47727	.46578	.45468	.44397	.43363
68 ..	.55554	.54196	.52885	.51619	.50398	.49218	.48079	.46978	.45915	.44887
69 ..	.56976	.55640	.54349	.53102	.51896	.50731	.49603	.48513	.47458	.46438
70 ..	.58407	.57095	.55826	.54598	.53410	.52260	.51147	.50069	.49025	.48013
71 ..	.59848	.58561	.57316	.56109	.54940	.53808	.52710	.51646	.50615	.49614
72 ..	.61294	.60035	.58815	.57632	.56484	.55371	.54291	.53243	.52225	.51237
73 ..	.62741	.61512	.60318	.59160	.58035	.56943	.55882	.54851	.53849	.52876
74 ..	.64183	.62983	.61818	.60686	.59586	.58516	.57476	.56464	.55480	.54523
75 ..	.65612	.64444	.63309	.62204	.61129	.60083	.59065	.58074	.57109	.56169
76 ..	.67026	.65891	.64786	.63710	.62661	.61640	.60646	.59676	.58731	.57810
77 ..	.68423	.67321	.66248	.65201	.64181	.63186	.62215	.61269	.60345	.59444
78 ..	.69800	.68733	.67692	.66676	.65684	.64717	.63772	.62849	.61948	.61068
79 ..	.71156	.70124	.69116	.68132	.67170	.66230	.65312	.64414	.63537	.62680
80 ..	.72487	.71490	.70516	.69563	.68632	.67721	.66830	.65959	.65106	.64272
81 ..	.73791	.72830	.71890	.70970	.70069	.69188	.68325	.67481	.66654	.65844
82 ..	.75065	.74140	.73235	.72348	.71479	.70628	.69794	.68977	.68176	.67391
83 ..	.76308	.75419	.74548	.73695	.72858	.72037	.71232	.70443	.69669	.68909
84 ..	.77516	.76664	.75828	.75008	.74203	.73413	.72638	.71877	.71130	.70396
85 ..	.78689	.77873	.77072	.76285	.75512	.74753	.74008	.73275	.72556	.71849

Age	4.2%	4.4%	4.6%	4.8%	5.0%	5.2%	5.4%	5.6%	5.8%	6.0%
86 ..	.79825	.79044	.78278	.77524	.76783	.76055	.75340	.74636	.73944	.73264
87 ..	.80921	.80176	.79443	.78722	.78014	.77316	.76630	.75956	.75292	.74638
88 ..	.81978	.81268	.80569	.79880	.79203	.78536	.77880	.77234	.76598	.75971
89 ..	.82994	.82317	.81651	.80995	.80349	.79712	.79085	.78467	.77859	.77259
90 ..	.83967	.83324	.82690	.82065	.81450	.80843	.80244	.79655	.79073	.78500
91 ..	.84898	.84288	.83685	.83091	.82505	.81928	.81358	.80795	.80241	.79693
92 ..	.85787	.85208	.84636	.84072	.83515	.82966	.82423	.81888	.81360	.80838
93 ..	.86632	.86083	.85541	.85006	.84477	.83955	.83440	.82931	.82428	.81931
94 ..	.87435	.86915	.86402	.85894	.85393	.84898	.84409	.83925	.83447	.82975
95 ..	.88197	.87705	.87219	.86739	.86265	.85795	.85331	.84872	.84419	.83970
96 ..	.88915	.88451	.87991	.87537	.87088	.86643	.86203	.85768	.85338	.84912
97 ..	.89593	.89154	.88720	.88290	.87865	.87444	.87028	.86616	.86208	.85804
98 ..	.90232	.89818	.89408	.89002	.88600	.88202	.87808	.87418	.87031	.86649
99 ..	.90835	.90444	.90057	.89674	.89294	.88918	.88546	.88177	.87811	.87449
100	.91397	.91028	.90663	.90301	.89942	.89587	.89234	.88885	.88539	.88196
101	.91930	.91583	.91238	.90897	.90558	.90223	.89890	.89560	.89233	.88908
102	.92424	.92096	.91771	.91448	.91128	.90811	.90496	.90184	.89875	.89568
103	.92914	.92605	.92300	.91996	.91695	.91397	.91100	.90806	.90514	.90225
104	.93364	.93074	.92786	.92501	.92217	.91935	.91656	.91379	.91103	.90830
105	.93809	.93537	.93266	.92998	.92731	.92467	.92204	.91943	.91683	.91426
106	.94365	.94115	.93867	.93621	.93376	.93133	.92892	.92651	.92413	.92176
107	.94994	.94771	.94549	.94328	.94108	.93890	.93673	.93457	.93242	.93028
108	.96010	.95830	.95651	.95472	.95295	.95118	.94942	.94767	.94593	.94420
109	.97985	.97893	.97801	.97710	.97619	.97529	.97438	.97348	.97259	.97170

Age	6.2%	6.4%	6.6%	6.8%	7.0%	7.2%	7.4%	7.6%	7.8%	8.0%
0 ...	.02534	.02370	.02223	.02093	.01978	.01874	.01782	.01699	.01625	.01559
1 ...	.01989	.01817	.01664	.01528	.01406	.01298	.01202	.01115	.01037	.00967
2 ...	.02061	.01882	.01722	.01580	.01454	.01340	.01239	.01148	.01066	.00993
3 ...	.02156	.01969	.01802	.01654	.01521	.01403	.01297	.01201	.01115	.01038
4 ...	.02264	.02069	.01896	.01741	.01602	.01478	.01367	.01267	.01176	.01095
5 ...	.02383	.02180	.01999	.01838	.01693	.01563	.01446	.01341	.01246	.01161
6 ...	.02512	.02301	.02113	.01944	.01793	.01657	.01535	.01424	.01325	.01235
7 ...	.02650	.02430	.02234	.02058	.01900	.01758	.01630	.01514	.01410	.01315
8 ...	.02798	.02570	.02365	.02182	.02017	.01868	.01734	.01613	.01503	.01404
9 ...	.02957	.02720	.02507	.02316	.02143	.01988	.01848	.01721	.01606	.01502
10 ..	.03128	.02881	.02659	.02460	.02280	.02118	.01971	.01838	.01718	.01608
11 ..	.03309	.03053	.02823	.02615	.02428	.02258	.02105	.01966	.01839	.01725

Age	6.2%	6.4%	6.6%	6.8%	7.0%	7.2%	7.4%	7.6%	7.8%	8.0%
12	.03503	.03237	.02997	.02781	.02585	.02408	.02248	.02103	.01971	.01850
13	.03704	.03428	.03179	.02954	.02750	.02565	.02398	.02246	.02108	.01982
14	.03909	.03623	.03364	.03130	.02918	.02726	.02551	.02392	.02248	.02116
15	.04117	.03820	.03551	.03308	.03087	.02886	.02704	.02538	.02387	.02249
16	.04324	.04016	.03737	.03484	.03254	.03046	.02855	.02682	.02524	.02379
17	.04533	.04214	.03924	.03661	.03422	.03205	.03007	.02826	.02661	.02509
18	.04746	.04415	.04114	.03841	.03592	.03366	.03159	.02970	.02798	.02639
19	.04963	.04620	.04309	.04025	.03766	.03530	.03315	.03117	.02937	.02772
20	.05191	.04835	.04512	.04217	.03948	.03702	.03478	.03272	.03083	.02910
21	.05427	.05058	.04723	.04416	.04137	.03881	.03647	.03432	.03235	.03054
22	.05672	.05291	.04943	.04625	.04334	.04067	.03823	.03599	.03394	.03205
23	.05930	.05535	.05174	.04844	.04542	.04265	.04010	.03777	.03562	.03364
24	.06204	.05795	.05421	.05078	.04764	.04476	.04211	.03967	.03743	.03536
25	.06497	.06074	.05687	.05331	.05005	.04705	.04429	.04174	.03940	.03724
26	.06811	.06373	.05972	.05603	.05264	.04952	.04665	.04400	.04155	.03929
27	.07146	.06694	.06278	.05895	.05543	.05219	.04920	.04644	.04389	.04153
28	.07503	.07036	.06605	.06209	.05844	.05507	.05196	.04908	.04642	.04396
29	.07881	.07398	.06953	.06542	.06163	.05814	.05490	.05191	.04913	.04656
30	.08279	.07780	.07319	.06894	.06502	.06138	.05802	.05491	.05202	.04933
31	.08697	.08182	.07707	.07267	.06860	.06483	.06134	.05810	.05509	.05229
32	.09137	.08606	.08115	.07660	.07239	.06848	.06485	.06148	.05835	.05543
33	.09601	.09053	.08546	.08075	.07639	.07234	.06858	.06508	.06182	.05878
34	.10084	.09520	.08996	.08511	.08059	.07640	.07249	.06886	.06547	.06231
35	.10590	.10009	.09470	.08968	.08501	.08067	.07662	.07285	.06933	.06605
36	.11120	.10522	.09966	.09448	.08966	.08517	.08098	.07706	.07341	.06999
37	.11674	.11059	.10486	.09952	.09454	.08990	.08556	.08150	.07771	.07416
38	.12254	.11621	.11032	.10481	.09968	.09487	.09039	.08618	.08225	.07856
39	.12857	.12208	.11601	.11035	.10505	.10009	.09545	.09110	.08702	.08320
40	.13487	.12820	.12196	.11613	.11067	.10555	.10076	.09626	.09204	.08807
41	.14142	.13458	.12817	.12217	.11655	.11127	.10632	.10167	.09730	.09319
42	.14823	.14122	.13464	.12848	.12269	.11725	.11214	.10734	.10282	.09856
43	.15535	.14816	.14141	.13508	.12913	.12353	.11826	.11330	.10863	.10422
44	.16274	.15538	.14847	.14196	.13585	.13008	.12466	.11954	.11472	.11016
45	.17042	.16290	.15581	.14914	.14286	.13694	.13135	.12608	.12110	.11640
46	.17842	.17073	.16348	.15664	.15020	.14411	.13836	.13293	.12780	.12294
47	.18672	.17886	.17145	.16445	.15784	.15159	.14568	.14010	.13481	.12980
48	.19534	.18732	.17974	.17258	.16581	.15940	.15334	.14759	.14215	.13699
49	.20429	.19612	.18838	.18106	.17413	.16757	.16134	.15544	.14984	.14453
50	.21362	.20529	.19740	.18993	.18284	.17612	.16974	.16368	.15793	.15247
51	.22332	.21484	.20680	.19917	.19194	.18506	.17853	.17232	.16642	.16080

Age	6.2%	6.4%	6.6%	6.8%	7.0%	7.2%	7.4%	7.6%	7.8%	8.0%
52 ..	.23341	.22479	.21660	.20883	.20144	.19442	.18774	.18138	.17533	.16957
53 ..	.24388	.23513	.22681	.21889	.21136	.20419	.19737	.19087	.18467	.17876
54 ..	.25473	.24585	.23739	.22935	.22168	.21437	.20741	.20076	.19442	.18837
55 ..	.26593	.25693	.24835	.24017	.23238	.22494	.21784	.21105	.20458	.19838
56 ..	.27742	.26831	.25962	.25132	.24340	.23583	.22860	.22169	.21508	.20875
57 ..	.28922	.28001	.27121	.26280	.25476	.24707	.23971	.23267	.22593	.21947
58 ..	.30129	.29199	.28309	.27457	.26642	.25862	.25114	.24398	.23712	.23053
59 ..	.31367	.30428	.29529	.28667	.27842	.27051	.26293	.25565	.24867	.24197
60 ..	.32638	.31691	.30784	.29914	.29079	.28278	.27509	.26771	.26062	.25380
61 ..	.33940	.32987	.32073	.31195	.30352	.29542	.28763	.28015	.27295	.26603
62 ..	.35269	.34311	.33391	.32506	.31656	.30837	.30050	.29293	.28564	.27862
63 ..	.36625	.35663	.34738	.33847	.32990	.32165	.31370	.30604	.29867	.29155
64 ..	.38007	.37043	.36113	.35218	.34356	.33524	.32723	.31950	.31204	.30484
65 ..	.39417	.38451	.37519	.36620	.35753	.34917	.34110	.33330	.32577	.31850
66 ..	.40871	.39905	.38972	.38071	.37201	.36361	.35550	.34765	.34006	.33273
67 ..	.42365	.41400	.40468	.39567	.38696	.37853	.37038	.36250	.35487	.34749
68 ..	.43892	.42931	.42001	.41101	.40230	.39387	.38570	.37780	.37014	.36272
69 ..	.45450	.44493	.43567	.42670	.41800	.40958	.40141	.39350	.38582	.37837
70 ..	.47033	.46083	.45162	.44269	.43403	.42563	.41748	.40957	.40189	.39443
71 ..	.48644	.47702	.46788	.45901	.45040	.44203	.43391	.42602	.41835	.41090
72 ..	.50278	.49347	.48441	.47562	.46707	.45877	.45069	.44284	.43520	.42776
73 ..	.51930	.51010	.50115	.49245	.48399	.47575	.46774	.45994	.45234	.44494
74 ..	.53591	.52684	.51802	.50943	.50106	.49291	.48497	.47724	.46970	.46235
75 ..	.55253	.54361	.53492	.52645	.51820	.51015	.50230	.49465	.48719	.47991
76	.56912	.56036	.55182	.54349	.53536	.52742	.51968	.51213	.50475	.49754
77 ..	.58565	.57706	.56868	.56050	.55251	.54471	.53708	.52964	.52236	.51525
78 ..	.60209	.59369	.58549	.57747	.56963	.56197	.55448	.54715	.53999	.53298
79 ..	.61841	.61021	.60219	.59435	.58668	.57917	.57182	.56463	.55760	.55071
80 ..	.63456	.62657	.61875	.61109	.60359	.59625	.58906	.58202	.57512	.56836
81 ..	.65050	.64273	.63512	.62766	.62034	.61318	.60616	.59927	.59252	.58590
82 ..	.66621	.65867	.65127	.64401	.63690	.62992	.62308	.61636	.60977	.60330
83 ..	.68164	.67433	.66716	.66012	.65321	.64642	.63976	.63322	.62680	.62050
84 ..	.69676	.68969	.68275	.67593	.66923	.66265	.65618	.64983	.64358	.63745
85 ..	.71154	.70472	.69801	.69141	.68493	.67856	.67229	.66613	.66007	.65412
86 ..	.72595	.71937	.71290	.70654	.70028	.69412	.68806	.68210	.67623	.67046
87 ..	.73995	.73362	.72740	.72127	.71523	.70929	.70344	.69768	.69201	.68642
88 ..	.75354	.74746	.74148	.73558	.72978	.72406	.71842	.71287	.70739	.70200
89 ..	.76668	.76085	.75511	.74945	.74387	.73837	.73295	.72761	.72234	.71714
90 ..	.77934	.77377	.76827	.76284	.75749	.75222	.74701	.74188	.73681	.73181
91 ..	.79153	.78620	.78094	.77575	.77063	.76558	.76059	.75566	.75080	.74600

Age	6.2%	6.4%	6.6%	6.8%	7.0%	7.2%	7.4%	7.6%	7.8%	8.0%
92 ..	.80323	.79814	.79312	.78816	.78326	.77843	.77365	.76894	.76428	.75967
93 ..	.81440	.80956	.80477	.80004	.79536	.79074	.78618	.78166	.77721	.77280
94 ..	.82508	.82047	.81591	.81140	.80694	.80253	.79817	.79387	.78961	.78539
95 ..	.83526	.83088	.82654	.82225	.81800	.81380	.80965	.80554	.80148	.79746
96 ..	.84491	.84074	.83662	.83254	.82850	.82450	.82055	.81663	.81276	.80892
97 ..	.85405	.85009	.84617	.84230	.83846	.83466	.83089	.82717	.82348	.81982
98 ..	.86270	.85895	.85523	.85155	.84791	.84430	.84072	.83718	.83367	.83019
99 ..	.87090	.86735	.86382	.86033	.85687	.85345	.85005	.84668	.84335	.84004
100	.87856	.87519	.87185	.86854	.86526	.86201	.85878	.85559	.85242	.84927
101	.88587	.88268	.87952	.87638	.87327	.87019	.86713	.86409	.86109	.85810
102	.89263	.88961	.88662	.88364	.88069	.87777	.87487	.87199	.86913	.86629
103	.89938	.89653	.89370	.89089	.88810	.88534	.88259	.87987	.87717	.87448
104	.90558	.90289	.90021	.89756	.89492	.89231	.88971	.88713	.88456	.88202
105	.91170	.90916	.90664	.90413	.90164	.89917	.89672	.89428	.89186	.88945
106	.91940	.91706	.91474	.91242	.91013	.90784	.90558	.90332	.90108	.89885
107	.92816	.92605	.92395	.92186	.91978	.91772	.91567	.91362	.91159	.90957
108	.94247	.94075	.93904	.93734	.93565	.93396	.93229	.93062	.92895	.92730
109	.97081	.96992	.96904	.96816	.96729	.96642	.96555	.96468	.96382	.96296

Age	8.2%	8.4%	8.6%	8.8%	9.0%	9.2%	9.4%	9.6%	9.8%	10.0%
0	.01498	.01444	.01395	.01351	.01310	.01273	.01240	.01209	.01181	.01155
1	.00904	.00847	.00796	.00749	.00707	.00668	.00633	.00601	.00572	.00545
2	.00926	.00866	.00812	.00763	.00718	.00677	.00640	.00606	.00575	.00547
3	.00968	.00905	.00848	.00796	.00748	.00705	.00666	.00630	.00597	.00567
4	.01021	.00955	.00894	.00839	.00789	.00744	.00702	.00664	.00629	.00597
5	.01083	.01013	.00949	.00891	.00839	.00790	.00746	.00706	.00669	.00635
6	.01153	.01080	.01012	.00951	.00895	.00844	.00798	.00755	.00715	.00679
7	.01229	.01151	.01081	.01016	.00957	.00903	.00854	.00808	.00767	.00728
8	.01314	.01232	.01157	.01089	.01026	.00969	.00917	.00869	.00825	.00784
9	.01407	.01321	.01242	.01170	.01104	.01044	.00989	.00938	.00891	.00848
10 ..	.01509	.01418	.01335	.01259	.01190	.01126	.01068	.01014	.00965	.00919
11 ..	.01620	.01525	.01437	.01358	.01285	.01218	.01156	.01099	.01047	.00998
12 ..	.01740	.01640	.01549	.01465	.01388	.01317	.01252	.01192	.01137	.01086
13 ..	.01867	.01762	.01665	.01577	.01496	.01422	.01353	.01290	.01231	.01177
14 ..	.01995	.01885	.01784	.01691	.01606	.01527	.01455	.01389	.01327	.01270
15 ..	.02123	.02007	.01901	.01803	.01714	.01632	.01556	.01485	.01420	.01360
16 ..	.02247	.02126	.02015	.01913	.01818	.01732	.01652	.01578	.01509	.01446
17 ..	.02371	.02244	.02127	.02020	.01921	.01830	.01746	.01668	.01596	.01529

Age	8.2%	8.4%	8.6%	8.8%	9.0%	9.2%	9.4%	9.6%	9.8%	10.0%
18 ..	.02494	.02361	.02239	.02126	.02022	.01926	.01838	.01756	.01680	.01610
19 ..	.02620	.02480	.02352	.02234	.02125	.02024	.01931	.01844	.01764	.01690
20 ..	.02751	.02605	.02471	.02346	.02232	.02126	.02028	.01937	.01853	.01775
21 ..	.02888	.02735	.02593	.02463	.02343	.02231	.02128	.02032	.01944	.01861
22 ..	.03030	.02870	.02722	.02585	.02458	.02341	.02233	.02132	.02038	.01951
23 ..	.03181	.03013	.02858	.02714	.02581	.02458	.02344	.02237	.02139	.02047
24 ..	.03345	.03169	.03006	.02855	.02715	.02586	.02465	.02353	.02249	.02152
25 ..	.03524	.03340	.03169	.03010	.02863	.02727	.02600	.02482	.02373	.02270
26 ..	.03720	.03527	.03348	.03181	.03027	.02884	.02750	.02626	.02510	.02402
27 ..	.03934	.03732	.03544	.03370	.03208	.03057	.02916	.02786	.02664	.02549
28 ..	.04167	.03955	.03759	.03576	.03406	.03247	.03099	.02962	.02833	.02713
29 ..	.04417	.04196	.03990	.03798	.03619	.03453	.03298	.03153	.03017	.02890
30 ..	.04684	.04452	.04237	.04036	.03848	.03674	.03510	.03358	.03215	.03081
31 ..	.04969	.04727	.04501	.04291	.04094	.03911	.03739	.03579	.03428	.03287
32 ..	.05272	.05019	.04783	.04563	.04357	.04165	.03984	.03816	.03657	.03509
33 ..	.05595	.05331	.05085	.04854	.04639	.04437	.04248	.04070	.03904	.03748
34 ..	.05936	.05661	.05403	.05162	.04936	.04725	.04527	.04341	.04166	.04001
35 ..	.06297	.06010	.05741	.05489	.05253	.05032	.04824	.04629	.04445	.04272
36 ..	.06679	.06380	.06100	.05837	.05590	.05358	.05140	.04935	.04742	.04561
37 ..	.07083	.06771	.06479	.06204	.05947	.05704	.05476	.05261	.05059	.04868
38 ..	.07511	.07186	.06881	.06595	.06326	.06072	.05834	.05609	.05397	.05196
39 ..	.07961	.07623	.07306	.07007	.06726	.06462	.06212	.05977	.05754	.05544
40 ..	.08434	.08083	.07753	.07442	.07149	.06873	.06612	.06366	.06133	.05913
41 ..	.08932	.08568	.08225	.07901	.07596	.07308	.07035	.06778	.06534	.06304
42 ..	.09455	.09077	.08720	.08384	.08066	.07766	.07481	.07213	.06958	.06717
43 ..	.10007	.09615	.09245	.08895	.08564	.08251	.07955	.07674	.07408	.07156
44 ..	.10586	.10180	.09796	.09433	.09089	.08763	.08454	.08162	.07884	.07621
45 ..	.11195	.10774	.10376	.09999	.09642	.09303	.08982	.08677	.08387	.08112
46 ..	.11835	.11400	.10987	.10596	.10225	.09873	.09539	.09222	.08920	.08633
47 ..	.12505	.12055	.11629	.11224	.10839	.10474	.10126	.09796	.09482	.09182
48 ..	.13209	.12745	.12303	.11884	.11485	.11106	.10746	.10402	.10075	.09764
49 ..	.13948	.13469	.13013	.12579	.12167	.11774	.11400	.11043	.10703	.10379
50 ..	.14727	.14233	.13762	.13314	.12887	.12481	.12093	.11723	.11370	.11033
51 ..	.15546	.15037	.14551	.14089	.13648	.13228	.12826	.12443	.12077	.11726
52 ..	.16407	.15884	.15384	.14907	.14452	.14018	.13603	.13206	.12826	.12463
53 ..	.17312	.16774	.16260	.15769	.15300	.14852	.14423	.14012	.13620	.13243
54 ..	.18259	.17707	.17179	.16674	.16191	.15729	.15286	.14862	.14456	.14067
55 ..	.19247	.18680	.18139	.17620	.17123	.16648	.16192	.15755	.15335	.14933
56 ..	.20270	.19690	.19135	.18602	.18092	.17603	.17134	.16684	.16251	.15836
57 ..	.21329	.20736	.20167	.19622	.19099	.18596	.18114	.17650	.17205	.16777

Age	8.2%	8.4%	8.6%	8.8%	9.0%	9.2%	9.4%	9.6%	9.8%	10.0%
58 ..	.22422	.21816	.21235	.20677	.20140	.19625	.19130	.18653	.18195	.17754
59 ..	.23553	.22935	.22341	.21770	.21221	.20693	.20185	.19696	.19225	.18772
60 ..	.24725	.24095	.23489	.22906	.22345	.21805	.21285	.20783	.20300	.19834
61 ..	.25937	.25296	.24679	.24084	.23511	.22959	.22427	.21914	.21419	.20941
62 ..	.27185	.26534	.25906	.25300	.24716	.24153	.23609	.23084	.22577	.22088
63 ..	.28469	.27808	.27169	.26553	.25959	.25384	.24830	.24294	.23776	.23275
64 ..	.29789	.29119	.28471	.27845	.27240	.26656	.26091	.25544	.25016	.24504
65 ..	.31148	.30468	.29812	.29177	.28563	.27969	.27394	.26837	.26299	.25777
66 ..	.32564	.31877	.31213	.30570	.29948	.29345	.28761	.28195	.27647	.27115
67 ..	.34034	.33341	.32671	.32021	.31391	.30780	.30188	.29614	.29057	.28517
68 ..	.35552	.34855	.34179	.33523	.32887	.32270	.31671	.31089	.30524	.29976
69 ..	.37115	.36414	.35734	.35073	.34432	.33809	.33204	.32616	.32045	.31489
70 ..	.38719	.38016	.37332	.36668	.36023	.35396	.34786	.34193	.33616	.33054
71 ..	.40366	.39662	.38977	.38311	.37663	.37032	.36419	.35821	.35240	.34674
72 ..	.42053	.41350	.40665	.39998	.39349	.38716	.38100	.37500	.36916	.36346
73 ..	.43774	.43073	.42389	.41723	.41074	.40441	.39824	.39222	.38636	.38063
74 ..	.45519	.44821	.44140	.43476	.42829	.42197	.41580	.40979	.40391	.39818
75 ..	.47280	.46587	.45910	.45250	.44605	.43975	.43360	.42759	.42173	.41599
76 ..	.49051	.48364	.47693	.47037	.46396	.45770	.45158	.44560	.43975	.43403
77 ..	.50830	.50150	.49486	.48836	.48201	.47580	.46972	.46377	.45795	.45225
78 ..	.52613	.51942	.51286	.50644	.50015	.49400	.48797	.48208	.47630	.47064
79 ..	.54396	.53736	.53089	.52456	.51835	.51227	.50632	.50048	.49476	.48915
80 ..	.56174	.55525	.54888	.54265	.53653	.53054	.52466	.51890	.51325	.50770
81 ..	.57941	.57305	.56681	.56068	.55467	.54878	.54299	.53731	.53174	.52627
82 ..	.59696	.59073	.58461	.57861	.57272	.56693	.56125	.55566	.55018	.54480
83 ..	.61430	.60822	.60224	.59637	.59061	.58494	.57937	.57389	.56851	.56322
84 ..	.63142	.62549	.61966	.61393	.60830	.60276	.59731	.59196	.58669	.58150
85 ..	.64825	.64249	.63682	.63124	.62575	.62035	.61503	.60980	.60465	.59958
86 ..	.66477	.65918	.65367	.64825	.64291	.63765	.63248	.62738	.62236	.61741
87 ..	.68092	.67550	.67016	.66490	.65972	.65462	.64959	.64463	.63975	.63493
88 ..	.69669	.69145	.68628	.68119	.67618	.67123	.66635	.66154	.65680	.65212
89 ..	.71201	.70696	.70198	.69706	.69221	.68742	.68270	.67805	.67345	.66892
90 ..	.72688	.72201	.71721	.71246	.70779	.70317	.69861	.69411	.68966	.68528
91 ..	.74126	.73658	.73196	.72739	.72289	.71844	.71404	.70970	.70541	.70117
92 ..	.75513	.75063	.74620	.74181	.73748	.73320	.72897	.72479	.72066	.71657
93 ..	.76844	.76414	.75988	.75568	.75152	.74741	.74334	.73932	.73535	.73142
94 ..	.78123	.77711	.77303	.76901	.76502	.76108	.75718	.75332	.74951	.74573
95 ..	.79348	.78954	.78565	.78179	.77798	.77421	.77047	.76677	.76312	.75950
96 ..	.80513	.80137	.79765	.79397	.79032	.78671	.78314	.77960	.77610	.77263
97 ..	.81621	.81262	.80908	.80556	.80208	.79864	.79522	.79184	.78849	.78517

Age	8.2%	8.4%	8.6%	8.8%	9.0%	9.2%	9.4%	9.6%	9.8%	10.0%
98 ..	.82674	.82333	.81995	.81660	.81328	.80999	.80673	.80351	.80031	.79713
99 ..	.83677	.83352	.83030	.82711	.82395	.82082	.81771	.81463	.81158	.80855
100	.84616	.84307	.84001	.83697	.83396	.83097	.82801	.82507	.82216	.81927
101	.85514	.85221	.84930	.84641	.84355	.84070	.83788	.83509	.83231	.82956
102	.86348	.86069	.85792	.85517	.85245	.84974	.84706	.84439	.84175	.83912
103	.87182	.86918	.86655	.86395	.86136	.85880	.85625	.85372	.85121	.84872
104	.87950	.87699	.87450	.87203	.86957	.86713	.86471	.86231	.85992	.85755
105	.88706	.88468	.88232	.87998	.87765	.87534	.87304	.87076	.86849	.86624
106	.89664	.89444	.89225	.89008	.88792	.88577	.88364	.88152	.87941	.87731
107	.90756	.90557	.90358	.90160	.89964	.89768	.89574	.89380	.89188	.88997
108	.92565	.92401	.92238	.92075	.91914	.91753	.91592	.91433	.91274	.91116
109	.96211	.96125	.96041	.95956	.95872	.95788	.95704	.95620	.95537	.95455

Age	10.2%	10.4%	10.6%	10.8%	11.0%	11.2%	11.4%	11.6%	11.8%	12.0%
0 ...	.01132	.01110	.01089	.01071	.01053	.01037	.01022	.01008	.00995	.00983
1 ...	.00520	.00497	.00476	.00457	.00439	.00423	.00407	.00393	.00379	.00367
2 ...	.00521	.00496	.00474	.00454	.00435	.00417	.00401	.00385	.00371	.00358
3 ...	.00539	.00513	.00490	.00468	.00447	.00429	.00411	.00395	.00380	.00366
4 ...	.00567	.00540	.00515	.00492	.00470	.00450	.00432	.00414	.00398	.00383
5 ...	.00603	.00574	.00547	.00523	.00500	.00478	.00459	.00440	.00423	.00407
6 ...	.00646	.00615	.00587	.00560	.00536	.00513	.00492	.00472	.00453	.00436
7 ...	.00693	.00660	.00630	.00602	.00576	.00551	.00529	.00508	.00488	.00469
8 ...	.00747	.00712	.00680	.00650	.00622	.00596	.00572	.00549	.00528	.00509
9 ...	.00808	.00771	.00737	.00705	.00675	.00648	.00622	.00598	.00576	.00555
10 ..	.00877	.00838	.00801	.00767	.00736	.00707	.00679	.00654	.00630	.00608
11 ..	.00954	.00912	.00873	.00838	.00804	.00773	.00744	.00717	.00692	.00668
12 ..	.01038	.00994	.00953	.00915	.00880	.00847	.00816	.00788	.00761	.00735
13 ..	.01127	.01081	.01038	.00998	.00960	.00925	.00893	.00862	.00833	.00806
14 ..	.01217	.01168	.01122	.01080	.01040	.01003	.00969	.00937	.00906	.00878
15 ..	.01305	.01253	.01205	.01160	.01118	.01079	.01042	.01008	.00976	.00946
16 ..	.01387	.01333	.01282	.01234	.01190	.01149	.01110	.01074	.01040	.01009
17 ..	.01467	.01409	.01356	.01306	.01259	.01216	.01175	.01137	.01101	.01067
18 ..	.01544	.01484	.01427	.01374	.01325	.01279	.01236	.01195	.01157	.01122
19 ..	.01621	.01557	.01497	.01442	.01390	.01341	.01295	.01253	.01213	.01175
20 ..	.01702	.01634	.01571	.01512	.01457	.01406	.01357	.01312	.01270	.01230
21 ..	.01784	.01713	.01646	.01584	.01526	.01471	.01420	.01372	.01327	.01285
22 ..	.01870	.01794	.01724	.01658	.01596	.01539	.01485	.01434	.01386	.01342
23 ..	.01961	.01881	.01807	.01737	.01672	.01611	.01554	.01500	.01449	.01402

Age	10.2%	10.4%	10.6%	10.8%	11.0%	11.2%	11.4%	11.6%	11.8%	12.0%
24 ..	.02062	.01977	.01899	.01825	.01756	.01691	.01630	.01573	.01520	.01469
25 ..	.02175	.02085	.02002	.01924	.01851	.01782	.01718	.01657	.01600	.01547
26 ..	.02301	.02207	.02119	.02036	.01958	.01886	.01817	.01753	.01692	.01635
27 ..	.02443	.02343	.02250	.02162	.02080	.02003	.01930	.01862	.01798	.01737
28 ..	.02600	.02495	.02396	.02303	.02216	.02134	.02057	.01985	.01916	.01852
29 ..	.02771	.02660	.02555	.02457	.02365	.02278	.02197	.02120	.02047	.01979
30 ..	.02956	.02838	.02728	.02624	.02526	.02434	.02348	.02266	.02189	.02116
31 ..	.03155	.03031	.02914	.02804	.02701	.02604	.02512	.02425	.02344	.02266
32 ..	.03370	.03239	.03115	.02999	.02890	.02787	.02690	.02598	.02511	.02429
33 ..	.03601	.03463	.03333	.03210	.03095	.02985	.02883	.02785	.02693	.02606
34 ..	.03847	.03701	.03564	.03434	.03312	.03197	.03088	.02985	.02887	.02795
35 ..	.04109	.03956	.03811	.03675	.03546	.03424	.03308	.03199	.03096	.02998
36 ..	.04390	.04228	.04076	.03932	.03795	.03667	.03545	.03429	.03320	.03216
37 ..	.04688	.04518	.04358	.04206	.04062	.03926	.03798	.03676	.03560	.03450
38 ..	.05007	.04829	.04660	.04500	.04349	.04205	.04069	.03940	.03818	.03701
39 ..	.05346	.05158	.04981	.04812	.04653	.04502	.04358	.04222	.04092	.03969
40 ..	.05705	.05508	.05321	.05144	.04976	.04817	.04666	.04522	.04385	.04255
41 ..	.06086	.05879	.05683	.05497	.05320	.05152	.04993	.04841	.04697	.04559
42 ..	.06488	.06271	.06066	.05870	.05684	.05508	.05340	.05180	.05028	.04882
43 ..	.06917	.06690	.06474	.06269	.06074	.05888	.05711	.05543	.05382	.05229
44 ..	.07370	.07132	.06906	.06691	.06486	.06291	.06105	.05928	.05759	.05598
45 ..	.07850	.07602	.07365	.07139	.06924	.06719	.06524	.06338	.06160	.05990
46 ..	.08360	.08100	.07852	.07616	.07390	.07176	.06970	.06775	.06587	.06409
47 ..	.08897	.08626	.08367	.08120	.07884	.07659	.07443	.07238	.07041	.06853
48 ..	.09466	.09183	.08912	.08654	.08407	.08172	.07946	.07730	.07524	.07326
49 ..	.10069	.09774	.09492	.09222	.08964	.08717	.08481	.08255	.08038	.07831
50 ..	.10711	.10403	.10109	.09827	.09558	.09300	.09053	.08816	.08589	.08371
51 ..	.11392	.11072	.10765	.10472	.10191	.09921	.09663	.09415	.09178	.08950
52 ..	.12116	.11783	.11464	.11159	.10866	.10585	.10315	.10057	.09808	.09569
53 ..	.12883	.12538	.12206	.11889	.11584	.11291	.11010	.10740	.10481	.10231
54 ..	.13694	.13336	.12992	.12662	.12345	.12041	.11748	.11467	.11196	.10936
55 ..	.14547	.14176	.13820	.13478	.13149	.12832	.12528	.12235	.11953	.11682
56 ..	.15437	.15054	.14685	.14330	.13989	.13661	.13345	.13040	.12747	.12464
57 ..	.16365	.15969	.15588	.15221	.14868	.14527	.14199	.13883	.13578	.13284
58 ..	.17330	.16921	.16528	.16149	.15783	.15431	.15091	.14763	.14447	.14141
59 ..	.18335	.17914	.17508	.17117	.16739	.16375	.16023	.15684	.15356	.15039
60 ..	.19385	.18952	.18534	.18131	.17741	.17365	.17001	.16650	.16311	.15982
61 ..	.20480	.20035	.19605	.19189	.18788	.18400	.18025	.17662	.17311	.16971
62 ..	.21615	.21158	.20717	.20290	.19877	.19477	.19090	.18716	.18354	.18003
63 ..	.22791	.22323	.21870	.21431	.21007	.20596	.20198	.19812	.19439	.19077

Age	10.2%	10.4%	10.6%	10.8%	11.0%	11.2%	11.4%	11.6%	11.8%	12.0%
64 ..	.24009	.23530	.23066	.22616	.22181	.21758	.21349	.20953	.20568	.20195
65 ..	.25271	.24781	.24306	.23846	.23400	.22967	.22547	.22139	.21744	.21360
66 ..	.26600	.26100	.25615	.25145	.24688	.24245	.23814	.23396	.22990	.22596
67 ..	.27992	.27483	.26989	.26509	.26043	.25590	.25150	.24722	.24306	.23901
68 ..	.29443	.28926	.28423	.27934	.27459	.26997	.26548	.26110	.25685	.25271
69 ..	.30950	.30424	.29914	.29417	.28934	.28463	.28005	.27559	.27125	.26703
70 ..	.32508	.31976	.31459	.30955	.30464	.29986	.29520	.29067	.28625	.28194
71 ..	.34122	.33585	.33062	.32552	.32054	.31570	.31097	.30637	.30187	.29749
72 ..	.35790	.35249	.34721	.34205	.33703	.33213	.32734	.32268	.31812	.31367
73 ..	.37505	.36960	.36428	.35909	.35403	.34908	.34425	.33953	.33492	.33042
74 ..	.39258	.38711	.38177	.37655	.37145	.36647	.36160	.35684	.35219	.34764
75 ..	.41039	.40491	.39956	.39432	.38921	.38420	.37931	.37452	.36983	.36525
76 ..	.42843	.42296	.41760	.41236	.40724	.40222	.39731	.39250	.38779	.38318
77 ..	.44668	.44122	.43588	.43065	.42552	.42050	.41559	.41077	.40605	.40143
78 ..	.46510	.45967	.45435	.44914	.44403	.43902	.43411	.42930	.42458	.41995
79 ..	.48365	.47826	.47298	.46780	.46271	.45773	.45284	.44804	.44333	.43871
80 ..	.50226	.49693	.49169	.48655	.48150	.47655	.47169	.46692	.46224	.45763
81 ..	.52090	.51562	.51044	.50536	.50036	.49546	.49064	.48590	.48125	.47668
82 ..	.53951	.53431	.52920	.52418	.51924	.51439	.50963	.50494	.50033	.49580
83 ..	.55802	.55291	.54788	.54294	.53808	.53329	.52859	.52396	.51941	.51493
84 ..	.57640	.57139	.56645	.56159	.55681	.55210	.54747	.54291	.53843	.53401
85 ..	.59459	.58968	.58484	.58008	.57539	.57077	.56623	.56175	.55733	.55298
86 ..	.61254	.60774	.60302	.59836	.59377	.58925	.58479	.58040	.57607	.57180
87 ..	.63019	.62551	.62090	.61635	.61187	.60745	.60309	.59880	.59456	.59038
88 ..	.64751	.64296	.63847	.63405	.62968	.62537	.62112	.61693	.61279	.60871
89 ..	.66444	.66003	.65567	.65137	.64712	.64293	.63880	.63471	.63068	.62670
90 ..	.68094	.67667	.67244	.66827	.66415	.66009	.65607	.65210	.64818	.64431
91 ..	.69699	.69285	.68877	.68473	.68074	.67680	.67291	.66906	.66526	.66150
92 ..	.71254	.70855	.70460	.70071	.69685	.69304	.68928	.68555	.68187	.67823
93 ..	.72753	.72369	.71989	.71613	.71242	.70874	.70510	.70150	.69794	.69442
94 ..	.74200	.73830	.73464	.73103	.72745	.72390	.72040	.71693	.71350	.71010
95 ..	.75591	.75236	.74885	.74538	.74194	.73853	.73516	.73182	.72851	.72524
96 ..	.76920	.76580	.76243	.75909	.75579	.75252	.74928	.74607	.74289	.73974
97 ..	.78188	.77863	.77540	.77220	.76904	.76590	.76279	.75971	.75665	.75363
98 ..	.79399	.79088	.78779	.78473	.78170	.77869	.77571	.77276	.76983	.76693
99 ..	.80555	.80257	.79962	.79670	.79380	.79092	.78807	.78525	.78244	.77966
100	.81641	.81357	.81075	.80796	.80518	.80243	.79971	.79700	.79432	.79165
101	.82683	.82412	.82144	.81877	.81612	.81350	.81089	.80831	.80574	.80320
102	.83652	.83394	.83137	.82882	.82630	.82379	.82130	.81883	.81637	.81394
103	.84624	.84379	.84135	.83892	.83652	.83413	.83176	.82941	.82707	.82475

Age	10.2%	10.4%	10.6%	10.8%	11.0%	11.2%	11.4%	11.6%	11.8%	12.0%
104	.85519	.85285	.85053	.84822	.84593	.84365	.84139	.83915	.83692	.83470
105	.86400	.86178	.85957	.85737	.85519	.85302	.85087	.84873	.84660	.84449
106	.87523	.87316	.87110	.86905	.86702	.86500	.86299	.86099	.85900	.85703
107	.88806	.88617	.88429	.88242	.88055	.87870	.87686	.87502	.87320	.87139
108	.90958	.90802	.90646	.90490	.90336	.90182	.90028	.89876	.89724	.89573
109	.95372	.95290	.95208	.95126	.95045	.94964	.94883	.94803	.94723	.94643

Age	12.2%	12.4%	12.6%	12.8%	13.0%	13.2%	13.4%	13.6%	13.8%	14.0%
0	.00972	.00961	.00951	.00941	.00932	.00924	.00916	.00908	.00901	.00894
1	.00355	.00345	.00334	.00325	.00316	.00307	.00299	.00292	.00285	.00278
2	.00346	.00334	.00323	.00313	.00303	.00294	.00286	.00278	.00270	.00263
3	.00353	.00340	.00329	.00318	.00307	.00298	.00289	.00280	.00272	.00264
4	.00369	.00356	.00343	.00332	.00321	.00310	.00300	.00291	.00283	.00274
5	.00392	.00377	.00364	.00352	.00340	.00329	.00318	.00308	.00299	.00290
6	.00420	.00405	.00391	.00377	.00365	.00353	.00342	.00331	.00321	.00311
7	.00452	.00436	.00421	.00406	.00393	.00380	.00368	.00357	.00346	.00336
8	.00490	.00473	.00457	.00441	.00427	.00413	.00400	.00388	.00376	.00365
9	.00535	.00517	.00499	.00483	.00467	.00453	.00439	.00426	.00413	.00402
10 ..	.00587	.00567	.00548	.00531	.00514	.00499	.00484	.00470	.00456	.00444
11 ..	.00645	.00624	.00605	.00586	.00568	.00551	.00536	.00521	.00506	.00493
12 ..	.00711	.00689	.00668	.00648	.00629	.00611	.00595	.00579	.00563	.00549
13 ..	.00781	.00757	.00735	.00714	.00694	.00675	.00657	.00640	.00624	.00609
14 ..	.00851	.00826	.00802	.00780	.00759	.00739	.00720	.00702	.00684	.00668
15 ..	.00918	.00891	.00866	.00842	.00820	.00799	.00779	.00759	.00741	.00724
16 ..	.00979	.00950	.00924	.00899	.00875	.00853	.00832	.00811	.00792	.00774
17 ..	.01035	.01006	.00978	.00951	.00926	.00902	.00880	.00859	.00838	.00819
18 ..	.01088	.01057	.01027	.00999	.00973	.00948	.00924	.00901	.00880	.00860
19 ..	.01139	.01106	.01075	.01045	.01017	.00990	.00965	.00942	.00919	.00898
20 ..	.01192	.01157	.01124	.01092	.01063	.01035	.01008	.00983	.00959	.00936
21 ..	.01245	.01208	.01173	.01139	.01108	.01078	.01050	.01023	.00998	.00974
22 ..	.01300	.01260	.01222	.01187	.01154	.01122	.01092	.01064	.01037	.01011
23 ..	.01357	.01315	.01275	.01238	.01202	.01168	.01137	.01106	.01078	.01051
24 ..	.01422	.01377	.01334	.01294	.01257	.01221	.01187	.01155	.01124	.01095
25 ..	.01496	.01448	.01403	.01361	.01320	.01282	.01246	.01212	.01180	.01149
26 ..	.01582	.01531	.01483	.01438	.01395	.01354	.01316	.01279	.01244	.01211
27 ..	.01680	.01626	.01575	.01527	.01481	.01437	.01396	.01357	.01320	.01285
28 ..	.01791	.01734	.01679	.01628	.01579	.01533	.01489	.01447	.01408	.01370
29 ..	.01914	.01853	.01795	.01740	.01688	.01639	.01592	.01548	.01505	.01465

Age	12.2%	12.4%	12.6%	12.8%	13.0%	13.2%	13.4%	13.6%	13.8%	14.0%
30 ..	.02048	.01982	.01921	.01862	.01807	.01754	.01704	.01657	.01612	.01569
31 ..	.02193	.02124	.02058	.01996	.01937	.01881	.01828	.01777	.01729	.01683
32 ..	.02351	.02278	.02208	.02142	.02079	.02019	.01962	.01908	.01857	.01808
33 ..	.02523	.02445	.02371	.02300	.02234	.02170	.02109	.02052	.01997	.01944
34 ..	.02707	.02624	.02545	.02470	.02399	.02331	.02267	.02205	.02146	.02091
35 ..	.02905	.02817	.02733	.02653	.02577	.02505	.02436	.02371	.02308	.02249
36 ..	.03117	.03024	.02935	.02850	.02769	.02693	.02619	.02550	.02483	.02419
37 ..	.03345	.03246	.03151	.03061	.02976	.02894	.02816	.02742	.02671	.02603
38 ..	.03590	.03485	.03385	.03289	.03198	.03112	.03029	.02950	.02874	.02802
39 ..	.03852	.03740	.03634	.03533	.03436	.03344	.03256	.03172	.03092	.03015
40 ..	.04131	.04013	.03900	.03793	.03690	.03593	.03499	.03410	.03324	.03242
41 ..	.04428	.04303	.04184	.04070	.03962	.03858	.03759	.03664	.03573	.03486
42 ..	.04744	.04612	.04486	.04366	.04250	.04140	.04035	.03934	.03838	.03745
43 ..	.05083	.04943	.04810	.04683	.04561	.04444	.04333	.04226	.04123	.04025
44 ..	.05443	.05296	.05155	.05021	.04892	.04768	.04650	.04537	.04428	.04324
45 ..	.05827	.05672	.05523	.05381	.05245	.05114	.04989	.04869	.04754	.04643
46 ..	.06237	.06074	.05917	.05767	.05623	.05485	.05352	.05225	.05103	.04986
47 ..	.06673	.06500	.06335	.06177	.06025	.05879	.05739	.05605	.05475	.05351
48 ..	.07137	.06955	.06781	.06614	.06454	.06300	.06152	.06010	.05874	.05742
49 ..	.07632	.07441	.07258	.07082	.06913	.06750	.06595	.06444	.06300	.06161
50 ..	.08162	.07962	.07769	.07584	.07407	.07236	.07071	.06913	.06760	.06614
51 ..	.08731	.08520	.08318	.08124	.07937	.07757	.07583	.07416	.07256	.07101
52 ..	.09340	.09119	.08907	.08703	.08507	.08317	.08135	.07959	.07790	.07627
53 ..	.09991	.09760	.09538	.09324	.09118	.08919	.08728	.08543	.08365	.08193
54 ..	.10685	.10443	.10211	.09987	.09771	.09562	.09361	.09167	.08980	.08799
55 ..	.11420	.11168	.10925	.10690	.10464	.10246	.10035	.09832	.09635	.09445
56 ..	.12191	.11928	.11675	.11430	.11193	.10965	.10745	.10531	.10325	.10126
57 ..	.13001	.12727	.12462	.12207	.11960	.11721	.11491	.11268	.11052	.10843
58 ..	.13846	.13561	.13286	.13020	.12762	.12513	.12273	.12040	.11814	.11595
59 ..	.14732	.14436	.14150	.13873	.13605	.13346	.13095	.12851	.12616	.12388
60 ..	.15665	.15358	.15060	.14772	.14494	.14224	.13962	.13709	.13463	.13225
61 ..	.16642	.16324	.16016	.15717	.15428	.15147	.14875	.14611	.14355	.14107
62 ..	.17663	.17333	.17014	.16704	.16404	.16113	.15830	.15556	.15290	.15031
63 ..	.18726	.18385	.18055	.17734	.17423	.17121	.16828	.16544	.16267	.15999
64 ..	.19833	.19481	.19140	.18809	.18487	.18175	.17871	.17576	.17289	.17010
65 ..	.20987	.20624	.20273	.19931	.19598	.19275	.18961	.18656	.18358	.18069
66 ..	.22213	.21840	.21478	.21125	.20783	.20449	.20125	.19809	.19501	.19202
67 ..	.23508	.23125	.22753	.22390	.22037	.21694	.21360	.21034	.20716	.20407
68 ..	.24868	.24476	.24094	.23722	.23359	.23006	.22662	.22327	.22000	.21681
69 ..	.26291	.25889	.25498	.25117	.24745	.24383	.24030	.23685	.23349	.23020

Age	12.2%	12.4%	12.6%	12.8%	13.0%	13.2%	13.4%	13.6%	13.8%	14.0%
70 ..	.27773	.27364	.26964	.26574	.26194	.25823	.25461	.25107	.24762	.24425
71 ..	.29321	.28904	.28496	.28099	.27710	.27331	.26961	.26599	.26246	.25900
72 ..	.30933	.30508	.30094	.29689	.29294	.28907	.28530	.28160	.27799	.27446
73 ..	.32602	.32171	.31751	.31340	.30938	.30545	.30160	.29784	.29416	.29056
74 ..	.34319	.33884	.33458	.33042	.32634	.32236	.31845	.31463	.31089	.30723
75 ..	.36076	.35637	.35207	.34786	.34374	.33970	.33575	.33188	.32808	.32437
76 ..	.37867	.37425	.36991	.36567	.36151	.35744	.35344	.34953	.34569	.34192
77 ..	.39690	.39245	.38810	.38383	.37964	.37554	.37151	.36756	.36369	.35989
78 ..	.41541	.41096	.40659	.40231	.39811	.39398	.38993	.38596	.38206	.37823
79 ..	.43418	.42973	.42536	.42107	.41686	.41272	.40866	.40467	.40075	.39691
80 ..	.45311	.44868	.44432	.44003	.43582	.43169	.42763	.42363	.41971	.41585
81 ..	.47219	.46777	.46343	.45916	.45497	.45084	.44679	.44280	.43888	.43502
82 ..	.49135	.48696	.48265	.47841	.47424	.47014	.46610	.46213	.45822	.45437
83 ..	.51052	.50618	.50191	.49771	.49357	.48950	.48549	.48154	.47766	.47383
84 ..	.52966	.52537	.52115	.51700	.51291	.50887	.50490	.50099	.49714	.49334
85 ..	.54870	.54448	.54032	.53622	.53218	.52820	.52428	.52041	.51660	.51284
86 ..	.56759	.56344	.55935	.55532	.55135	.54742	.54356	.53974	.53598	.53227
87 ..	.58626	.58219	.57818	.57422	.57031	.56646	.56266	.55891	.55521	.55155
88 ..	.60468	.60070	.59677	.59290	.58907	.58529	.58157	.57788	.57425	.57066
89 ..	.62277	.61888	.61505	.61126	.60753	.60383	.60018	.59658	.59302	.58950
90 ..	.64048	.63670	.63296	.62927	.62563	.62202	.61846	.61494	.61146	.60803
91 ..	.65778	.65411	.65048	.64689	.64334	.63983	.63636	.63293	.62954	.62619
92 ..	.67462	.67106	.66754	.66406	.66061	.65720	.65383	.65050	.64720	.64393
93 ..	.69094	.68749	.68408	.68071	.67737	.67406	.67079	.66756	.66435	.66118
94 ..	.70673	.70340	.70011	.69685	.69362	.69042	.68725	.68412	.68102	.67794
95 ..	.72199	.71878	.71560	.71246	.70934	.70625	.70319	.70016	.69716	.69419
96 ..	.73662	.73353	.73047	.72743	.72443	.72145	.71850	.71557	.71268	.70981
97 ..	.75063	.74766	.74471	.74180	.73890	.73604	.73319	.73038	.72758	.72482
98 ..	.76405	.76120	.75837	.75557	.75279	.75003	.74730	.74459	.74190	.73923
99 ..	.77690	.77417	.77146	.76877	.76610	.76345	.76083	.75822	.75564	.75308
100	.78901	.78639	.78379	.78121	.77866	.77612	.77360	.77110	.76862	.76616
101	.80067	.79816	.79568	.79321	.79076	.78832	.78591	.78351	.78114	.77877
102	.81152	.80912	.80674	.80438	.80203	.79970	.79738	.79508	.79280	.79054
103	.82245	.82016	.81789	.81563	.81339	.81116	.80895	.80676	.80458	.80241
104	.83250	.83031	.82814	.82599	.82384	.82171	.81960	.81750	.81541	.81334
105	.84239	.84030	.83823	.83617	.83412	.83209	.83006	.82806	.82606	.82407
106	.85507	.85311	.85117	.84924	.84733	.84542	.84352	.84164	.83976	.83790
107	.86958	.86779	.86600	.86422	.86246	.86070	.85895	.85721	.85548	.85376
108	.89422	.89272	.89123	.88974	.88826	.88679	.88533	.88386	.88241	.88096
109	.94563	.94484	.94405	.94326	.94248	.94170	.94092	.94014	.93937	.93860